BREAKING AWAY

HOW GREAT LEADERS CREATE INNOVATION THAT DRIVES SUSTAINABLE GROWTH —AND WHY OTHERS FAIL

JANE STEVENSON
BILAL KAAFARANI

New York   Chicago   San Francisco   Lisbon   London   Madrid   Mexico City
Milan   New Delhi   San Juan   Seoul   Singapore   Sydney   Toronto

The **McGraw·Hill** Companies

1 2 3 4 5 6 7 8 9 10 11 12 13 14 15   QFR/QFR   1 9 8 7 6 5 4 3 2 1

ISBN   978-0-07-175394-4
MHID   0-07-175394-X

The opinions expressed in this book are solely those of the authors and do not represent those of The Coca-Cola Company.

Library of Congress Cataloging-in-Publication Data

Stevenson, Jane.
          Breaking away : how great leaders create innovation that drives sustainable growth—and why others fail / by Jane Stevenson, Bilal Kaafarani.
               p.   cm.
          Includes index.
          ISBN-13: 978-0-07-175394-4
          ISBN-10: 0-07-175394-X
          1. Creative ability in business.   2. Leadership.   3. New products.
     I. Kaafarani, Bilal.   II. Title.

     HD53.S737   2011
     658.4'092—dc22   2010047470

McGraw-Hill books are available at special quantity discounts to use as premiums and sales promotions or for use in corporate training programs. To contact a representative, please e-mail us at bulksales@mcgraw-hill.com.

This book is printed on acid-free paper.

We dedicate this book to:

*The glory of Almighty God, our Creator and
the Ultimate Leader of all innovation.*

*To our families,
whose constant love,
belief, support, and understanding
made it possible to write this book.*

*Thank you
from the bottom of our hearts
to our awesome spouses,
Janice and Alan,
and to our wonderful children:
Steven, Brian, Kristina, and Danielle;
Jonathan and Emily.
May the CEOs you work for
be leaders of innovation, growth, and possibility.
And to our parents,
Moussa and Jouheida Kaafarani, and
John and Nancy Edison,
with much love.*

Contents

Special Thanks

To Our Team

If it takes a village to raise a child, what does it take to raise a book? In our case, it took a Diana. While we developed the concepts, research, case studies, and ideas, Diana LaSalle gave them wings to fly. Diana, you have a special gift for taking even the most complex concepts and conveying them in a simple, yet intriguing way. Your belief in this project was unflagging, your commitment was passionate, and your support was a constant encouragement. We thank you for believing this book was special enough to set aside, at least briefly, your own identity as the bestselling coauthor of *Priceless: Turning Ordinary Products into Extraordinary Experiences* to collaborate and write with us. You were our partner in every respect. We thank you, Diana, for being the wind beneath our wings!

Jeffrey Smith, where do we begin? Without you, this book would never have happened. You were there from day one, and you never left our side for a moment. You were a friend, a counselor, a coach, a mentor, a brother, sometimes a handful, and always an inspiration. Thank you for making yourself endlessly available, no matter when we called you. From lending us your conference room for quiet space to helping us connect concepts to the right people and places to negotiating the contracts, you were an unbelievable support. Wherever we are, you are always with us. Thanks, Jeffrey, for believing in us. You are an amazing man!

Barbara Shear, you made it feel so easy to connect our ideas with a marketing plan. The doors open wide for you, and we had the privilege to share our ideas with some of the top publications in the world because of your credibility and leadership. Thanks so much for believing in us enough to volunteer your time and talent to *Breaking Away*. You are a dear friend!

Amy Rennert, from the first dinner we had together, you recognized that the concept for this project was special. The discussion and the interaction we had with you put us on the right road for the journey this book took. Thanks for patiently laboring with us to distill its message. You got us access to the best in the business. We appreciate your dedication and commitment!

Thank you, Jenny Williams, Pauline Williams, Michele Mullen-Hampton, and Kandi Thomas. You kept us on track, got us to the right cities, and constantly encouraged us. How lucky we are to have such great support from our teams! Special thanks to Jenny for the graphics and to Pauline for handling the endless release process.

Shereen Khundmiri, your talents took a fledging idea and turned it into a first-class website. We were so blessed to have you on our team. You brought first "The Winning Jaguar" and then "Breaking Away" to life and taught us so much. You are a joy to be around and top talent to boot. Thanks so much!

Emily, your willingness to draw the trademark for The Winning Jaguar, LLC, was a priceless gift. You are a real talent, honey, so special, smart, and beautiful!

Mary Glenn and the whole McGraw-Hill *Breaking Away* team, you were terrific. Thanks for taking the book to a higher level of thinking and delivery. Mary, you are a truly gifted editor, and we are so grateful to have had the opportunity to work with you on our first book. Thanks for believing in *Breaking Away* from your first reading of the proposal to its completion. You and your team are awesome to work with!

To Our Families
Janice, your endless support and constant belief in me made this project feel so much easier. Thirty-two years, and you're still the one!

Alan, your belief in the importance of this project and your willingness to pick up the slack at home to make it possible have been such a gift. Thank you for standing by me and for always seeing the best in me. I love you, darling!

Danielle, Jonathan, and Emily, thanks for sacrificing your time with us to make this book a reality. Your belief and your pride in what we were doing made us love you even more—if that's possible!

Mom and Dad Edison, you were behind us all the way, and your help saved the day on more than one occasion. A special thank you to you, Dad, for all the times you got the kids where they needed to be even before I had to ask—just because you're the amazing man you are.

Genet, thanks for your love and support and for helping me keep the Stevenson house a home even in the most chaotic times.

To Our Colleagues and Friends

Adrienne Fontanella, Pamela Day, Joseph Ciechanover, Michelle Betts, Beth Comstock, Denise Morrison, Cynthia McCague, and all Jane's friends from Prayerapy, Korn/Ferry, and Heidrick and Struggles, you will never know how much your enthusiasm and belief in this project meant to us. You are amazing friends and such an inspiration to us!

Melanie Kusin, Raja Rajamannar, Lauren Doliva, Lee Hanson, Sam Marks, and Stephen Miles, thanks so much for believing in us enough to introduce us to people you thought we should talk to for the book.

Terry Cobb, you have our gratitude for reading through multiple drafts and giving thoughtful suggestions, but most of all for sharing Diana with us for the better part of a year. The support and encouragement you gave her throughout the writing of the book are appreciated more than we can say.

Our most sincere thanks to the General Electric Company for opening up your innovation centers, exposing us to many of your top development projects, allowing us to participate in innovation reviews with Jeff Immelt and division leaders, and letting us spend time with some twenty-plus executives and project leaders across the company. And to Humana, where Bilal has had the wonderful opportunity to serve on the innovation advisory board and understand innovation from a completely different industry's perspective. Also to McCain Food, Merial, and the Estée Lauder Companies, where we were able to spend quality time interviewing multiple executives. Your generosity in opening your doors wide to allow us to live and learn with you was invaluable and provided deep perspectives.

Last, but certainly not least, thanks to The Coca-Cola Company and to Korn/Ferry International for supporting our desire to write this book. Special thanks to Korn/Ferry for dedicating resources, staff, and real commitment to forwarding the concepts presented here.

Acknowledgments

We cannot adequately express our gratitude to the people listed here for their willingness to spend time discussing innovation and leadership and for sharing their stories with us. Their validation of our innovation framework and the concepts in this book has been priceless! We only wish there were enough pages in this book to have shared all the insights, quotes, and experiences they shared with us.

Angela Ahrendts; chief executive officer; Burberry Group, plc

Prith Banerjee, Ph.D.; director, HP Labs/senior vice president, research; Hewlett-Packard

Ajay Banga; president and chief executive officer; MasterCard

Jose Barella; chief executive officer; Merial, Ltd.

Karen Basian; vice president, strategy, mergers/acquisitions and innovation; McCain Foods

Bruce Chizen; former chief executive officer; Adobe

Tim Clark; president; Emirates Airlines, Dubai (UAE)

Beth Comstock; senior vice president and chief marketing officer; General Electric

Jean-Michel Cossery; chief marketing officer; GE Healthcare

Peter Darbee; chairman, chief executive officer, and president; Pacific Gas and Electric Company

Ellen de Brabander; senior vice president, global research and development; Merial Ltd.

Mark Dudzinski; chief marketing officer; GE Energy

Cammie Dunaway; executive vice president, marketing and sales; Nintendo Americas

Zhang Fang; president; Non-Stop, Shanghai

Adrienne Fontanella; former executive vice president and group president; Mattel

Bill Ford; executive chairman; Ford Motor Company

Fabrizio Freda; president and chief executive officer; The Estée Lauder Companies

Veronique Gabai-Pinsky; global brand president; The Estée Lauder Companies

Harvey Gedeon; executive vice president, research and development, corporate product innovation; The Estée Lauder Companies

Martin Glenn; chief executive officer; Birds Eye/Iglo

Christina Gold; former chief executive officer; Western Union

Brian Goldner; president and chief executive officer; Hasbro Inc.

Yang Jin Guo; chief executive officer, president; ABC Financial Leasing Co., Ltd.

Betsy Holden; senior advisor; McKinsey; and former chief executive officer; Kraft USA

Eli Hurvitz; chairman of the board; Teva Pharmaceuticals

Mike Idelchik; vice president of advanced technologies; General Electric

Jeffrey Immelt; chairman and chief executive officer; General Electric

Bruno Jactel, D.V.M.; chief marketing officer; Merial Ltd.

Patrick Jarvis; manager, communications and public relations; GE Global Research

Marco Jesi; chairman of the board; Limoni Profumerie S.p.A.

B. I. Jianjun; deputy general manager; China Huadian Corporation

Dean Kamen; founder and chief executive officer; DEKA

Patrick Ko; managing director; FirsTrust, China

Mark Little; senior vice president, director of research centers; General Electric

Sam Marks; chief executive officer; Marks Worldwide

Murray Martin; chief executive officer and president; Pitney Bowes

Mike McCallister; chairman, chief executive officer, and president; Humana, Inc.

Sheri McCoy; worldwide chairman and chief executive officer; Johnson & Johnson Pharmaceuticals

Dale Morrison; chief executive officer and president; McCain Foods Limited

Denise Morrison; executive vice president, chief operating officer, and board member; The Campbell Soup Co.

Daria Myers; senior vice president, global innovation/sustainability; The Estée Lauder Companies

Isabel Noboa Ponton; founder and executive president; Consorcio Nobis

Dan Propper; chairman of the board, former chief executive officer; Food Processing/Osem Investments Ltd., Nestlé Osem

Baoyun Qiao; dean; China Academy of Public Finance and Policy

Raja Rajamannar; executive vice president, chief marketing and innovation officer; Humana, Inc.

T. P. Rao, Sr., Ph.D.; manager, international group nutrition division; Taiyo Kagaku Co. Ltd.

Michael Sands; chief executive officer; Balance Bar Co.

Brett Shevack; founder and chief executive officer; Brand Initiatives Group

Jeffrey Smith; principal shareholder, managing director; Greenberg and Traurig

Murat Ulker; chairman and chief executive officer; Yildiz Holdings

Liu Xinli; chief economist of state taxation; National Tax Bureau, Shanghai Municipal Administration

Jim Zaza; group president and chief marketing and strategy officer; Yildiz Holdings

Introduction

Every once in a while, you meet someone who brings a perfect counterpoint to your perspective. That's what happened to create this book. In 2006, Bilal Kaafarani's path crossed Jane Stevenson's while she was working on an assignment for The Coca-Cola Company. Tasked with finding a proven change agent to help revitalize the company's top-line growth with breakthrough commercial ideas, her search led her to Bilal. Not only did she find a successful candidate, she found a kindred spirit.

At their first meeting, Bilal and Jane discovered they both had goals of sharing their learning about innovation and leadership in a book—and that learning is extensive. As a global innovation executive with P&G, Kraft, FritoLay, and currently as an officer of The Coca-Cola Company, Bilal has experienced what is wrtten about in *Breaking Away* first hand. After his arrival, Coca-Cola was listed in *BusinessWeek*'s 2009 Top 25 Companies for Innovation for the first time in its history. Bilal was also honored by *BusinessWeek* as one of the world's Top 25 Masters of Innovation. He has had the unique opportunity to work with some of the best brands in the world and to experience the benefits and liabilities of many leadershp styles and environments.

Jane, Vice Chairman, Board and CEO Services at Korn/Ferry International, is an industry expert on recruiting leaders of growth and innovation. A pioneer in the field, she was responsible for bringing in many of the first chief innovation officers and CEOs who focused on growth through innovation. She is a marquee brand in her industry and was acknowledged in *BusinessWeek's* 100 Most Influential Search Consultants in the World for the past two years.

As Bilal and Jane continued to talk about writing together, it became clear that this was an innovation match of significant importance. Their shared insights provide a unique perspective for looking at the essence of what creates breakthrough innovations and the leaders who champion them. This perspective couldn't come at a better time. Innovation isn't just the decade's hottest topic; it is a business imperative. It's that elusive elixir that must be found to achieve sustainable growth and drive shareholder value. In fact, we would be hard-pressed to find an organization that isn't looking to develop, embed, or acquire innovation capabilities.

Unfortunately, many companies don't recognize the magnitude of the role leadership and cultural transformation play in reaching their desired outcomes. Instead, top executives often look for innovation processes and methodologies to drive success. They believe that the innovation gap is a technical one and that overlaying innovation processes on top of existing infrastructures will bring the growth they need. That's why it has traditionally been a common practice to bring in outside consultants to develop new processes or to make an existing leader in marketing, strategy, or research and development accountable for delivering company-wide innovation.

These practices may be accepted, but that doesn't make them right. We've found, time and again, that companies that have truly mastered innovation are driven by courageous leaders, leaders who understand that innovation and leadership are inextricably linked. The truth is, it's simply impossible to outsource responsibility for innovation to either an external consultant or an inside change agent. The accountability rests at the top. Think of it like a great symphony orchestra that needs a conductor. Even with a stage full of virtuosos, without the conductor, all you have is a bunch of talented musicians. With vision and leadership, however, you have a marvelous ensemble capable of creating a masterpiece.

It's the same in business. Like the conductor, the CEO lays out the vision, determines the best course of action, and decides how to use the talent under his or her command to the best advantage. While standing at the podium, the conductor understands that performers only hear their instruments from their spot in the concert hall, which is also true for the CEO. Only the maestro is able to listen to the collective group as it interacts with the environment and then set the tone to deliver an exceptional experience. What we envision is a future where leaders become legendary conductors and their companies virtuoso symphony orchestras. That's why we wrote *Breaking Away*.

While numerous books have been written about innovation processes and the environment that effective leadership provides, little has been said about how the two combine. That's the gap we want to fill. Leadership is the essence from which true innovation is conceived, but without the right cultural environment, the seeds of innovation can't bloom into commercial reality. It is this "magic" mix that enables some leaders to create a sustainable innovation engine fueled by everyone who works at their company, while others equally set on harnessing innovation's growth potential ultimately fail.

In *Breaking Away*, we'll look at why this happens and how to achieve different types of innovation success, including the risk profile that can stretch potential without mortgaging your future, quality parameters that will continually delight your customers, cultural factors essential in nurturing the right environment, and the leadership skills you need to bring out the best in your employees. We'll also define the unique ability that successful innovation leaders have to live at the intersection of business, technology, and customer insights, making it possible for their companies to win in the marketplace. As we move through these topics, we'll see and address a number of inherent contradictions—those between risk and reward, complexity and simplicity, the ultimate in empowerment and complete anarchy, and finally, security and the cost of doing nothing.

To ensure that our observations and theories are well qualified, we've talked with a broad range of CEOs and top executives who have either had substantial long-term innovation success or painfully learned from innovation failures. They come from every region and industry in the world. Traveling throughout the United States, we visited companies such as Ford, General Electric, Hewlett-Packard, MasterCard, The Estée Lauder Companies, Humana, and Pitney Bowes. We journeyed from Italy to Istanbul, from China to Mexico, and from Ecuador to Dubai. Throughout this book, we'll highlight some of the stories and insights CEOs and top executives shared with us and see not only where they've been, but where they hope to go. Unless otherwise noted, all quotes and corresponding case studies are from our interviews and conversations.

We have also analyzed the world's historical innovation leaders, believing there are invaluable lessons to be learned from those who laid the foundation for the world we live in today. People like Henry Ford, Herman Lay, and Thomas Edison (who is a part of Jane's lineage) will take us back to a time not unlike our own. Like ours, their world was full of change, possibility, technological breakthroughs, and risk. We'll take you step-by-step through some of their journeys to uncover how invention led to breakaway innovations that built empires. Along with the perspectives we've gained from them, our research, and our travels, we've converted our collective fifty-plus years of experience into key insights that provide platforms to create tremendous commercial success and energize environments that motivate and invigorate everyone.

Among these insights are the essential elements of innovation and an elegantly simple model that reveals four types of innovation that can lead to growth. Defined as transformational, category, marketplace, and operational, each level offers its own unique opportunities. These different types of innovation can take place at the societal, category, customer, or company levels and apply to different market conditions and time frames in a company's growth. This makes it possible to keep a continuous stream of innovation moving through a company to create maximum value.

Along with the different levels, we'll also explore leadership characteristics and the kind of environment that nurtures each type of innovation. These descriptions and some easy-to-follow models can help you better understand whether you have the right people in the right jobs. Finally, we talk about activating innovation in a way that reduces risk and increases the chances for success. At its heart, innovation is about how to break away from the pack and master the marketplace, using the best employees, technology, business heritage, and resources—all driven by the needs of the customer.

In the tradition of books like *In Search of Excellence* and *Good to Great*, which deliver insight and also give you the tools to act on it, we believe that by the time you turn the last page of *Breaking Away*, you'll be inspired and enthusiastically committed to implementing the principles discussed here. While profound, many of the most important elements in leading innovation are simple. Without conscious awareness and a good dose of humility, however, they can prove difficult to implement.

Our intention is to engage your intellect and awaken a sense of possibility from beginning to end. We want this book to be useful enough to become an ongoing reference in every organization's quest to be its best and to lead the way for others to achieve things they can only hope to accomplish in an environment of true innovation. We believe this path will forever change the way you think about innovation and leadership, and how innovation can help your company grow—now and for decades to come. The change starts now.

Do not go where the path may lead you;
go instead where there is no path
and leave a trail.

—RALPH WALDO EMERSON

PART 1

THE INNOVATION EQUATION

f there was ever a time when innovation needed to be a prime directive, it's in today's world. It's not like the old days, when consumers were filling up houses with their first Frigidaire or the garage with new Craftsman tools and a second car. It's the twenty-first century, and never before in human history have consumers been faced with such an abundance of goods and services, so many choices and so many ways to purchase. It's overwhelming, and for many people, accumulating possessions just isn't that important anymore. The reason for this attitude is simple. In much of the developed world, people have most of what they *need*, but what they *want* has changed. They're no longer at the bottom of Maslow's hierarchy of needs, where people have to deal with basic survival. They've evolved. People today crave emotional and spiritual engagement with what they buy.

In a 2007 report on consumer macro trends, the Hartman Group stated that redefining quality of life—not goods and services—would be the decade's leading market trend. For many companies, this new view of consumption has been hard to grasp. We're used to creating offerings that have a purpose, not thinking about how it will impact someone's life beyond performing a task. But it is making an impact, fulfilling that "want" that will drive innovation for decades to come.

The business world has changed too. Today's companies are being judged on a quarter-to-quarter basis, making true innovation more risky to leaders' careers than ever before. High visibility in the press, boardroom, and social media has everyone second-guessing everyone else, and no misstep or miscue—whether real or perceived—goes unnoticed for long. To make matters even trickier, the world financial climate isn't risk friendly, limiting once-relied-on sources of speculative money. That's not likely to change anytime soon. So we have consumers who want something that's hard to define and a business environment that undermines the security and opportunity we need to innovate.

And yet the demand for earth-shattering breakthroughs and innovation projects that drive sustainable growth is greater than ever. In fact, "innovate or die" has become the anthem for the twenty-first-century corporation. One executive asked us, "Is the business world in a death spiral?" While we hesitate to say yes, the truth is that many companies are facing a bleak future if they don't embrace innovation—even though the barriers to embracing it are significant.

The reason for this is threefold. First, we're living in a time in which the word *innovation* is often misused, abused, and even held up as a shield against taking risks. Much of the problem lies in the fact that there is no common language construct through which to discuss innovation. Because of this deficit, true innovation is often lost in innovation-speak, where people say one thing and do something else. Second is the lack of an internal framework for innovation that honors each company's distinct culture and way of doing business. Third, there's the matter of risk. Although finding ways to assess risk is the top issue for most CEOs, such methods have often been hard to come by.

In *Breaking Away*, we'll take you through a journey to address these issues and define innovation in a way that is understandable and useful in the real world. We'll also share insights we have gained from countless hours of discussion and debate while interviewing dozens of the world's top leaders. Along the way, we'll introduce a groundbreaking model that any company can use to explore innovation based on four distinct levels. We'll also show you how and where to find inspiration for breakthroughs of your own. Finally, we'll look at how to see risk in a new way and use it to shorten the leap from inspiration to commercial performance.

Innovation may be hard to define, but one thing is certain— you can't live without it. You also can't do it if you don't truly understand it. So what *is* innovation?

CHAPTER 1

This Is Innovation

A Rose by Any Other Name

> "Never before in history has innovation
> offered promise of so much
> to so many in so short a time."
>
> **—BILL GATES**

The year was 1752. Dark clouds filled the sky while a father and son walked across an isolated field toward a small shed. No one knew they were there or what they hoped to accomplish. If they succeeded, there would be time for that; if they failed, no one would be the wiser. As storm clouds gathered, the father launched his contraption—a kite with a string made of twine and an iron key attached to it by a length of nonconducting silk. Wrapping the silk around his hand, he watched the kite rise into the sky and waited.

One promising cloud after another passed. Just as they were about to give up, the father noticed some loose threads from the twine standing straight out like the excited hairs on the back of one's neck when something is about to happen. Curious, he moved his knuckles toward the dangling key, and an electric spark appeared. As rain soaked the cord, more sparks flew, and for the first time, Benjamin Franklin saw what he would later dub "electric fire."

Many have heard this story of Franklin and his famous kite. What most don't realize, however, is that he wasn't the first to prove the theory that electricity and lightning are one and the same. Unknown to him, French naturalist Thomas-François Dalibard, inspired by Franklin's writings, had beaten him to the punch a month before.[1] Within weeks of hearing the news, others throughout Europe repeated the same experiment. So why is Franklin remembered as the father of electricity, while the others are little more than a footnote? It's simple: unless discovery is followed by invention and innovation, even something as profound as electricity means little to the ordinary person. The reason we remember Ben Franklin is because, in addition to his discovery, he and others after him did something with it, and from these inventions came innovations that changed our world.

In this chapter, we'll begin to create a universal context for innovation—what distinguishes it from discovery and invention, what defines it, and what the key components are. We'll also look at the sequence for innovation, which starts with curiosity like Franklin's and evolves through experimentation, utilization, and adoption or social change. Finally, we'll reveal the real treasure—a model for innovation so simple and elegant in concept that it will change the way innovation is defined and how it's talked about in boardrooms, C-suites, and classrooms around the world. Along the way, we'll learn from some of history's greatest innovators and from leaders and companies who have mastered unique types of innovation in modern times. Their stories will help illustrate the workings of innovation and how you can harness it to change your own company in unimagined ways.

Discovery, Invention, and Innovation

One of the traps many people fall into when thinking about innovation is using the term interchangeably with its more celebrated cousins—*discovery* and *invention*. While all three share elements of "newness," they are essentially different branches of the same family tree. Understanding the difference between them is the first step toward simplifying innovation.

At the root is discovery. Driven by curiosity, human need, and insight, discovery uncovers something previously unknown or unrecognized. It's not just new; it's unimagined by all but the curious few. Franklin's discovery was exciting, but in truth, it was at first of little use to the general public. To make his discovery useful, it had to progress to invention.

Invention happens when something that is known—such as an idea about electricity—is turned into something new through experimentation. Franklin used his discovery to invent the first commercial application of electricity, the lightning rod. From there, others added their own insights to advance electricity and inspire a young Thomas Edison, who, more than a hundred years later, literally lit up the world.

Edison is often credited with "inventing" the light bulb, but the truth is no one person can claim that accomplishment. What Edison did was improve on a primitive, fifty-year-old light fixture by combining new materials and systems, thus creating the first practical incandescent light bulb. This achievement didn't happen overnight. In fact, it took years, a team of scientists, and more than nine hundred experiments that didn't work before finding the one that did.

In December 1879, Edison held the first public demonstration of his long-lasting light bulb in Menlo Park, New Jersey, where perhaps his most significant and least-known accomplishment was born: the world's first industrial research laboratory.

Set up specifically to produce constant technological innovation and improvement, it was home to an elite staff of engineers and researchers who, under Edison's direction, worked on the telephone, the phonograph, the electric railroad, and of course, the electric light bulb. By 1880, the facility was developing commercial electrical lighting components. Soon after, Edison opened his first factory to build the products conceived at Menlo Park. This was the beginning of the commercialization of the electric industry and the company we know today as General Electric.

This sequence—where discovery uncovers, invention creates, and innovation expands the idea into something customers want to buy—has been consistently repeated throughout history. Edison's genius was his ability to recognize this sequence and put it to work on a large scale. Throughout his life, he took on the task of "bringing good things to life" in a big way. Because he did, society changed, and the world was transformed.

Illumination, automobiles, telephones, and the Internet may all have been made *possible* because of invention, but they were made *available* through innovation. None of them would have existed without the harnessing of electricity. Can you trace your company's products and services back to Edison? Can you see the footprint of other great discoveries like the wheel, stone tools, or even cave paintings in your company's DNA? If you're an executive with John Deere, Home Depot, or Facebook, you'll find your history in these long-ago discoveries. Following the threads of your origins gives you a perspective you probably didn't have before. Recognizing the roots of innovation is the first step to seeing it all around you.

The Nature of Innovation

Virtually every business leader today would agree that understanding and mastering innovation is one of the most important challenges companies face. Innovation has been the subject of debate, discussion, study, and more than a few arguments over the past hundred years. So when we began to talk about innovation with business leaders, it wasn't surprising that no two thought about it in the same way.

Cammie Dunaway, executive vice president of marketing and sales for Nintendo Americas, describes it as "the point where consumer insight, market opportunity, and development of a product or service intersect." Ajay Banga, president and CEO of Master-Card, defines it as "an idea that is inherently scalable. If you can't scale it, it's not really innovation." Bill Ford, executive chairman of Ford Motor Company, simply says that innovation comprises "products and processes that make people's lives better."

None of these answers are right or wrong; they are just different. It's this difference in thinking about what innovation is that makes talking about it, maximizing it, and in some cases actually doing it confusing.

The reason for this confusion is tragically simple. Over time, the word has come to be used as an umbrella term for everything from true breakthroughs, like the hybrid car, to the modification of product features or processes that could then be labeled "new." Renovations are not innovations. Tweaking technology to make a product more current or loading it with features to keep up with the competition is not setting the bar any higher. To be a true innovation, a product, service, or company has to have three essential elements: **it has to be unique, it has to be valuable, and it has to be worthy of exchange**.

One of a Kind

Often when we think of innovation, we think in terms of "new" rather than "unique." It might seem like a small distinction, but in the world of innovation, it's huge. *Unique* means that, at the time of the innovation, it is one of a kind, the only one—no one has done it before. *New*, on the other hand, can mean anything from starting over to fresh or rejuvenated. To be innovative, you have to be unique.

Coming up with something unique in the field of animal health isn't always easy. It can take years, even decades, for science to advance a new technology and turn it into something useful on a big scale. Merial Ltd., a worldwide animal health company, almost made it look easy when they found a way to turn a molecule into a product that revolutionized the pet industry. Anyone who owns a cat or dog probably knows the name: Frontline.

For as long as anyone could remember, dealing with fleas was a messy and less than effective process. Shampoos, powders, and flea collars dominated the market. Even though the remedies didn't work for more than a few days, they were the only choices available. With its new Frontline science, Merial knew it had something very different. For the first time, pet owners could protect their animals by applying a drop of liquid on the back of their necks. Fleas died within twelve hours, and the reproduction cycle stopped. What's more, the effects lasted an entire month. If all went well, Merial was looking at a category killer. There was only one problem.

At the same time Frontline was being launched, another company was introducing its own product based on a different molecule. Each product offered unique benefits, but it was likely that only one would survive. So once again, Merial had to come up with something unique. This time, it was a marketing approach. "Since the product was a new method of flea control and needed to be sold at a premium price, we knew we had to educate pet owners quickly," says Bruno Jactel, Merial's chief marketing officer. "We were also dealing with the fact that people have a strong emotional attachment to their animals, so they needed to trust us. We adopted a two-prong approach, pushing product through professional distribution channels like veterinarians, while at the same time pulling the consumer in through direct marketing." It was an enormous success, not only for the company, but for vets, clinics, pet stores, and pharmacies as well.

Frontline was originally projected to be a $200 million product. By 2000, it was growing at 15–20 percent a year, and by 2007, it had hit the billion-dollar mark—something no other product of its kind has ever achieved.[2] The competitor didn't make it.

Definably Valuable

Frontline had several things going for it, not the least of which was the solution to a universal problem. It wasn't just its effectiveness that made it a success, however. "People care deeply about their animals," says Jactel. "So it was never just about taking care of a pest problem. Love and responsibility are factors too. In a way, it makes people feel good about themselves when they feel good about their pets." In other words, there is value beyond the monetary—and that's the second requirement for innovation. Defined as "the positive impact a product, service, or company has on a person's life," value is at the heart of innovation. In fact, by its very nature, innovation is meant to improve or enhance what is currently possible.

The Estée Lauder Companies built its business on helping women feel beautiful. It has done so primarily by focusing on both the art and the science of makeup and skin care. Its laboratories create products that address women's perceived, felt, and anticipated needs. Part of this process involves looking at fashion, the physiological and psychological issues of aging, and social trends. As product innovators, The Estée Lauder Companies is one of the best, but what really sets the company apart is the customer experience it provides.

"We want women to experience our products as they're meant to be used," says president and CEO Fabrizio Freda. "We want them to find their beauty. That's why our salespeople take the time to work with customers to help them look their best and then keep in touch with them to be their personal consultants. These associates serve as our market research. They are our direct links, our eyes and ears to deep consumer insights."

This philosophy of personal contact to gain consumer insight is how the company's innovation of a "customized shopping experience" came about. Sales associates are trained to quickly assess whether a woman wants to spend a few minutes picking up a product or half an hour on a makeup consultation. Nothing is assumed. Recognizing that not everyone shops in stores anymore, the company has also developed an education-loaded, interactive website that offers a virtual experience almost as rich as the real-world one. By staying closely in tune with its customers, the company makes sure it has the right solution for each woman's beauty needs.

For example, in 2010, the Estée Lauder brand's marketing department recognized how stressed women were about posting photographs on social networking sites. In response, it developed and launched a "Your Beauty, Your Style, Your Profile" event, where one of the company's celebrated makeup artists created a perfect look for each woman. A professional photographer then took a photo and e-mailed her a copy, so it could instantly be uploaded to her favorite site.

While these events were free to customers, the revenue generated through the purchase of makeup and skin care products used to create that special look were substantial. Nonetheless, the real value is the win-win situation such events create: women feel confident, beautiful, and valued, and the company continues to gain market share and foster enthusiasm for its products. "The customized shopping program has revolutionized the way we do business with our customers," says Freda. "This innovation ultimately changed our business model and dramatically improved customer satisfaction and sales per customer. It also changed the way our competitors now approach their business."

Worthy of Exchange

The third and often overlooked component of innovation is what we call being "worthy of exchange." When the first two elements are satisfied (you have something unique that delivers true value), then people are willing to give or exchange something in order to get what you have. This exchange is most easily defined as a monetary one, but it can also be intellectual, such as when universities or researchers share findings. It can also be emotional in the form of time, loyalty, and support, which happens when people get involved in charity programs such as the innovative Habitat for Humanity.

In business culture, however, commercial success—or at least a fighting chance to make money and a reasonable return on investment—is the standard by which we normally judge the viability of innovation. If it's not commercially successful or worthy of exchange, then it's not innovation. One of the best and most enduring examples of this principle goes back to the early twentieth century.

The idea for personalized vehicle travel had been in the minds of inventors since the 1300s, but it wasn't until the early days of the twentieth century that a viable product was developed. The man who took the concept from invention to innovation was Henry Ford, and his financial success didn't stem from his car being the most innovative. It came from the innovation of how he produced that car.

From the beginning, Ford dreamed of building an automobile that would mobilize the masses, freeing them to travel wherever and whenever they wanted. It was an admirable vision, one others shared, but it had one serious glitch—ordinary people couldn't afford the price of independence. The automobile was a toy for the wealthy and, by all accounts, would stay that way for some time to come. This prediction of upper-class driving domination didn't stop Ford. A true innovator, he decided that if ordinary people couldn't afford the car he could make at the time, he would just have to build a cheaper car.

By developing the assembly line and paying workers higher wages to keep them happy and productive, he dropped the price of a Model T from $1,000 to $400. Ford realized his dream, and America began mobilizing faster than even he could have imagined.

In 1920 alone, the Ford Motor Company churned out a million Model T cars. Each of them was reasonably priced, sensible, and durable, just as Ford had envisioned. Over the next several years, workers cranked out millions more of the conservative motorcars, and people continued to buy them.

Ford accomplished his goals by creating a *unique* manufacturing process and organizational structure, delivering previously unimagined *value* to his customers, and turning both into a commercial success (making a product *worthy of exchange*), making millions of dollars in the process. Today, Ford is the only American automaker to refuse government bailout money, and during what was arguably one of the worst financial periods in decades, posted a profit of $4.7 billion for the first half of 2010.[3] The company did it by returning to its innovation roots when everyone else was scrambling.

"During the dark days of the last few years, we increased funding for R&D," explains Bill Ford. "We made innovation a top priority, protected it to keep it alive and kicking, and accelerated product development to lead the industry." As a result, the company was able to introduce new designs and advance the development of the hybrid car. Creating affordable products that deliver freedom of the road to the masses is at the heart of Ford's "worthy of exchange" formula. Knowing why customers will part with their hard-earned money to take a chance on an innovation is not only invaluable to marketing and sales—sometimes it opens doors you never knew existed.

Innovation and the Four Levels

What is significant about what Ford did more than a hundred years ago isn't just that it mass-produced automobiles. The large-scale manufacturing innovation Henry Ford introduced literally changed the world and created enormous opportunity. Once a paradigm shifts, or *Transformational Innovation* occurs (as with the widespread production of affordable automobiles), the innovation can be developed more fully and expanded on to create whole new industries, markets, and ways of doing business.

For example, once people were no longer limited to traveling short distances, they saw the world in an entirely new way. They traveled for work, play, and commerce, coming together as never before. This mobility, in turn, created the need for roads, gas stations, auto repair, insurance, roadside lodging, and so on, giving birth to entire industries. Each of these came with its own set of follow-on innovations, opening up marketplace opportunities like billboard advertising and operational opportunities such as car dealerships and supply chains. All of this growth was made possible because of the Transformational Innovation that had already occurred—the affordable automobile.

When you look at it from this perspective, innovation becomes a very different animal. It's no longer just a big-game hunt, where world-changing breakthroughs are the only prize. There is treasure buried everywhere if you know where to look. To help you recognize and explore an expanded field of innovation opportunities, we've constructed a model that lists the defining characteristics and business attributes of four distinct types of innovation: transformational, category, marketplace, and operational. Each of these levels are viable and valuable. They are, however, remarkably different from one another, and their applications apply to different time frames and market conditions. It's important to determine which types of innovation can create maximum value for your company wherever it is in its life cycle.

TABLE 1.1 The Innovation Model

TRANSFORMATIONAL

DEFINING CHARACTERISTICS	BUSINESS ATTRIBUTES
Is driven by curiosity and discovery	Is difficult to define in terms of full market potential
Changes society and life as we know it	Has no defined P&L or timeline
Provides benefits to our culture and communities	Has a risk-reward ratio exponentially higher than any other type of innovation
Is disruptive and revolutionary in scope; is sustainable in dimension	Has an unclear adoption rate
Cascades into follow-on innovation at category, marketplace, and operational levels	Can't survive in a large corporate environment unless it's protected from standard success metrics
Becomes something we depend on	Provides a legacy instead of preserving the status quo
Focuses on right-brain thinking and creativity	

MARKETPLACE

DEFINING CHARACTERISTICS	BUSINESS ATTRIBUTES
Is driven by competitive market needs	Often achieves incremental revenue
Is generally defined by new features or benefits	Tends to be the most profitable
Creates new ways to delight the customer or consumer	Is fast to market
Impacts multiple categories	Doesn't have to be core product or service—can be an in-and-out proposition
Keeps category innovation fresh and current	Is exciting for everyone—company and customer
Is opportunistic and anticipates or creates market changes	Maximizes cross-functional participation
Focuses on left-brain creativity	Can impact business short term but also has long-term potential

CATEGORY

DEFINING CHARACTERISTICS	BUSINESS ATTRIBUTES
Is driven by understood or anticipated consumer or customer needs and insights	Has the potential to be profitable
Builds on or stems from Transformational Innovation	Has predictable revenue and timelines
Involves breakthrough of applications instead of invention	Fits well with Wall Street expectations
Is guided by a valid business case	Is often led by marketing more than technology
Allows for follow-on innovation at the marketplace and operational levels	Is most successful when there is fluid interaction between marketing and R&D
Focuses on left- and right-brain creativity	Has risks that are more manageable than those associated with transformational innovation

OPERATIONAL

DEFINING CHARACTERISTICS	BUSINESS ATTRIBUTES
Is driven by internal insights to deliver efficiency, effectiveness, and profitability for the business.	Focuses on how to improve the company's operations
Creates or changes organizational structure and processes	Is more detail oriented and metric focused
Brings efficiencies that benefit everyone	Is productivity driven
Improves work life	Allows for cost savings that can benefit the company or customer
Improves productivity	Improves the company's business case
Improves financial performance	Is oriented toward sustainability
Improves the customer experience through better processes	Has highly predictable financial returns
Focuses on left-brain thinking	Is the lowest-risk type of innovation and should always be utilized in every business

Transformational Innovation

This is the granddaddy of innovation. It is so big and so power-ful that others continue to build on it for generations. In fact, that's one of the hallmarks of Transformational Innovation—it's a disruptive breakthrough that changes society. Transforma-tional Innovation so impacts the way we live that, over time, we discover we can't thrive without it.

Some of what we've already talked about qualifies as Trans-formational Innovation, such as the light bulb and mass-produced automobiles. We know historically how these things have trans-formed society, and there probably isn't a CEO alive who wouldn't like to be at the helm when a transformational breakthrough finally takes hold. But the truth is it takes generations and the nurturing of successive CEOs to get there. Most of us will never come close to being a part of Transformational Innovation, but we still need to recognize it so we can take advantage of the pos-sibilities that already exist.

There is no doubt that the Internet has forever altered how we function in the world. It is the ultimate example of Trans-formational Innovation. Because of it, the way we think about life today is altogether different than the way we thought about it growing up. The Internet has changed the way we shop, listen to music, get our news, pay our bills, meet new friends, commu-nicate, travel, keep from getting lost, manage investments, play games, and even read books. It has spawned literally thousands of follow-on innovations, far beyond what anyone could have imagined when it was first conceived more than fifty years ago.

With its roots in a U.S. Department of Defense program called the Advanced Research Projects Agency (ARPA), the idea of the Internet began in the late 1950s. Described as a "future-oriented funder of high risk, high gain," the project laid the groundwork for what became known as ARPANET. At the time that ARPANET was established, there were fewer than ten thousand computers in the world, and they were enor-mously expensive. But the government was interested in seeing whether computers could communicate with each other through a common language and a common protocol. Using universities as their test subjects, they eventually succeeded. It would be eleven years before the first "node" was installed at the University of California–Los Angeles and another eight years before it evolved into what we know today as the Internet, but evolve it has. By the time the twenty-first century was a decade old, more than 1.2 billion people were reportedly connected in cyberspace.

For those who recognized the coming tidal wave, there was enormous opportunity to form new empires, spawning fantastic names—such as eBay, Amazon, Google, and Yahoo—and equally fantastic profits. These early adopters gambled that the Internet would engage the world, and they've been rewarded. For those who didn't recognize the potential impact, there was considerable pain as the brick-and-mortar world tried to find its footing on an increasingly cyber-run planet. Today it isn't a question of what the Internet can do; it's a question of how you can continue to use it, both for the opportunities it offers and the challenges it creates.

Category Innovation

While Transformational Innovation is revolutionary, you might say Category Innovation is evolutionary—or as Marco Jesi, chairman of the board of Limoni Profumerie, puts it, "It's something new and different from the past." Originating at the industry level and building off of Transformational Innovation that has already proven itself, category breakthroughs are generally found in the new application of ideas, products, or services rather than in the creation of inventions. This level of innovation is primarily market driven and geared toward meeting customer needs, often before customers even know the need is there.

Perhaps one of the best companies at keying in on the perceived, felt, or as yet unimagined needs of customers is Apple. Recognized as one of the most innovative companies of our time, it figures in many of our stories throughout this book—not so much for what it's done, but for why and how it's done it. Like many of the most innovative companies in history, Apple began with a passion—in this case, for technology.

Steve Jobs, one of Apple's founders, started college to please his parents, but as he told it in a commencement speech at Stanford University,[4] "After six months, I couldn't see the value in it. . . . I had no idea what I wanted to do with my life and no idea of how college was going to help me figure it out. . . . So I decided to drop out and trust that it would all work out OK. The minute I dropped out, I could stop taking the required classes that didn't interest me and begin dropping in on the ones that looked far more interesting. Much of what I stumbled into by following my curiosity and intuition turned out to be priceless later on."

He went on to recall that his school (Reed College) at that time offered perhaps the best calligraphy instruction in the country. Throughout the campus, every poster and every label on every drawer was beautifully hand calligraphed. It fascinated him, so he decided to take a calligraphy class. He learned about serif and sans serif typefaces, about varying the amount of space between different letter combinations, about what makes great typography great. He never dreamed it would have any practical application in his life, but ten years later, it did—in a big way. "When we were designing the first Macintosh computer, it all came back to me, and we designed it all into the Mac," he said. "It was the first computer with beautiful typography. If I had never dropped out, I would never have dropped in on that calligraphy class, and personal computers might not have the wonderful typography that they do."

The typeface developed for the Mac was later emulated by Microsoft and figured significantly in the initial product of another innovation company of the time—Adobe. It was a licensing agreement between Apple and Adobe for the Postscript printer language that introduced a new era in desktop printing.

In years to come, Apple's penchant for killer application of technology on an industry-wide scale would surface in the iMac, iPod, iPhone, and iPad. All of these products have cascaded into new categories. The iPod, developed from technology introduced for mp3 players, catapulted the music industry into a whole new era. Follow-on innovations like iTunes and must-have accessories resulted in billions of dollars for Apple. The iPhone has not only made billions more for the company, but it has also created a whole generation of independent, millionaire app developers.

The reason Apple is so successful is that it understands how to innovate from the outside in. It focuses first on what customers need—often before they know they need it—and takes advantage of Transformational and other Category Innovations, like the Internet and mp3 technology, to fuel its ideas. Time and again Apple has redefined categories, rightfully earning its legendary status.

Marketplace Innovation

As Category Innovation is building new industries, our next type of innovation is building or expanding new markets. Living in the realm of features, benefits, and sales, Marketplace Innovation is all about devising new ways to reach and delight the customer in engaging ways. By coming up with unique modifications for products, services, and delivery methods, its aim is to have a positive impact on people's lives. Everything from pop tops to the Magic Eraser qualifies as Marketplace Innovation, but our favorite story comes from the past, as much for its genius as for the lessons it can teach us about broadening our view and focusing on the wants, needs, and even whims of our customers.

We talked earlier about the insight of Henry Ford and how he found a way to make automobiles affordable by changing the way cars were made and companies were staffed. His innovations literally mobilized the world, but unfortunately, his vision had a slight flaw. To keep costs low, he determined that every car needed to be the same color, so every Ford rolling onto the new highways of an increasingly mobile society looked exactly the same—black and conservative. Ford saw no problem with this. After all, in his view, it was the affordability of the car that was important.

What he didn't count on was the fact that, in time, the sameness and sensibility would begin to wear thin with his customers. With wheels giving customers independence and the jobs Ford and a healthy transportation-related economy created giving them money in their pockets, the climate became ripe for a color takeover. Enter Alfred P. Sloan.

For several years, General Motors had been trying to no avail to break Ford's hold on the automobile industry. GM was already trying different Marketplace Innovations by offering various nameplates and new models with improved technology. But Ford's conservative cars had so penetrated the market that "inexpensive and sensible" became the standard against which all cars were judged. Add to that the fact that automobiles didn't wear out quickly, and GM knew it was fighting an uphill battle. In a departure from marketing thinking of the time, the company decided to look beyond the older-generation market that shared Ford's conservative values and focus instead on the modern, fun-loving, young driver—and Ford, without realizing it, gave GM the perfect opening.

It is widely agreed that at some point or other, Henry Ford muttered, "They can have any color they want, as long as it's black." Zeroing in on this, GM asked its allied company, DuPont, to create a complete palette of colored lacquers that would appeal to the younger demographic. The sexy hues, named Duco by the manufacturer, all but sealed Ford's fate.

The 1927 Chevrolet arrived on the scene with marvelously colored exteriors and lavish trim. No more boring black, no more looking like your parents. General Motors invited young drivers to break away from the ordinary in vivid greens and lemon yellows. For the first time, more people chose a GM product over a Ford. What's more, they paid a higher price. This came as a great personal disappointment to Ford, who genuinely believed that the basic principles of quality, reliability, and low price would keep his customers with him forever. What he failed to remember is that nothing stays the same. People evolve, and what they value also evolves. Without market agility, you can't sustain growth. This is a fact that the automaker should have paid attention to in the twenties, and it's certainly something we need to understand today.

Marketplace Innovation is and should be a continuous process. In fact, it's all around us. If you open your mind to it, you'll recognize it in environmentally friendly packaging such as the plant-derived, compostable bags that Frito-Lay developed for its Sun Chips and in processes like Home Depot's tracking software that looks up a purchase for customers who've lost their receipts. It's evident in the exploding number of apps for Apple's iPhone. And it's evident in Ford's innovative social-networking marketing program for the new Fiesta that launched in 2010.

Before the Fiesta arrived in dealerships, Ford asked one hundred twentysomethings to test it for six months and document their experiences. When the car hit the car lots, more than ten thousand people had already put in their orders. Like a blast from the past, the most popular color was Lime Squeeze.[5] The best innovators not only see the future, they also learn from the past and use these lessons to keep their products, services, and companies fresh. If you don't innovate continuously, someday you may find that even your most secure offerings are obsolete.

Operational Innovation

Obsolescence is something every company should fear, especially when it comes to this final form of innovation. Operational Innovation is more about the how of business than the what. Being efficient, up-to-date, and innovative in your processes, operations, and relationships is every bit as important as having a killer product or service. Every company and 100 percent of its workforce should be engaged in Operational Innovation at all times.

Whether it's about finding efficiencies that save time, improving quality, increasing productivity, improving the work environment, or upgrading technology to beat the competition, running a forward-moving, continually evolving company is essential for ongoing success. But like all types of innovation, Operational Innovation has to be tied to more than saving or making money; it has to benefit the customer as well. So even though this type of innovation has a primarily internal focus, it must never lose sight of the outside world of consumers and customers—the importance of which one bright kid recognized way ahead of the competition.

In the mid-1980s, the giants of the home computer market noticed and then dismissed a University of Texas dropout. They said his PCs Limited would never be a threat, and furthermore, his method of "hawking" PCs was "unbecoming a true tech company."[6] At that time, computers were sold only in stores, and customers were limited to features the manufacturer decided were relevant. It wasn't exactly one size fits all, but it was close.

The dropout was Michael Dell, and his remarkable Operational Innovation sent the computer market reeling. By mastering logistics and the supply chain, he combined components, processes, and materials in a way that had never been done in the computer world. The plan was to build computers to customers' specifications and then ship the product directly to them, eliminating the middleman. It worked better and faster than anyone imagined. No one could compete with Dell's prices, so he literally defined the terms of competition. In the process, he changed an industry. Within a short time, Dell had humbled companies like Hewlett-Packard (HP) and driven IBM out of the personal computer market.[7]

The most important thing Dell did was to take an operational approach to solving a consumer problem—in this case, the high cost of computers. His innovations weren't done just for the sake of saving money for his company; they were to make PCs more accessible to the public. This is an important distinction worth repeating: operational changes that are adopted solely to cut costs, without regard as to how those changes will impact the customer or advance the company, are not innovation. In fact, they often have deadly consequences.

In 2007, Circuit City fired its thirty-four hundred most experienced salespeople and replaced them with generic, untrained, near-minimum-wage workers. It announced this as a new era for the company. The retailer had built a reputation on helping consumers navigate the complexities of buying electronics, but after the cost-saving workforce initiative, the quality of its service declined so sharply that it put the company out of business in less than twenty-four months![8]

As much as Circuit City wanted to believe that what happened was the result of a declining economy, the fact is that it made many mistakes in its final brick-and-mortar years, not the least of which was a failure to innovate. We all know companies that became stagnant by living on past accomplishments. Michael Dell readily admits that he has not put enough emphasis on research and development (R&D) in the past decade and that his company dropped the ball when HP and others began luring customers into stores with sleek new models. The temptation to rest on your laurels when things are going well or to slash R&D budgets and focus primarily on cutting operational costs has gotten many companies into fiscal hot water. The way to avoid getting caught in this death spiral is to learn from the past, focus on the future, and literally go with the flow.

Cascading

Throughout this chapter, we've shared stories about companies, products, and services that illustrate the different components of innovation, from how it unfolds to its essential elements and the concept of four levels. The next piece of the innovation model is called *cascading*, and it defines how innovation not only exists on four levels but also flows from one level to the next like a waterfall.

To explain further, let's go back to electricity. Once electricity was harnessed, it enabled innovations to flow from transformational breakthroughs into categories like light bulb manufacturing, power companies, electric pole installation, and so on. These industries filled market needs that in turn led to Marketplace Innovations that supported the category or enabled companies to engage the customer through breakthroughs in packaging, specialized tools for electricians, animated store windows at Christmas, and even colorful neon signs. We could go on and on, but you see the pattern where one level builds and flows downward to the next.

It's also true that, occasionally, what goes down can also flow up. When Apple created the iPhone, it took what began as a Marketplace Innovation to enhance the market created by cell phones and catapulted the device to transformational status. Its tremendous success changed how people communicated and interacted with music and the Internet, helped break cultural barriers, and created endless opportunities for large and small developers to say, "There's an app for that!" It has even moved giants like Microsoft to abandon their fixation on Windows traditions and start from scratch to try and innovate their way back into smartphones.

Also taking the upwardly mobile path was Wal-Mart. When the company innovated its supply chain to link customers to vendors, it was able to deliver on its promise to provide unique value to the customer. As it expanded horizontally and vertically from clothing and appliances to food, gardening supplies, and pharmacies, it became impossible for other stores to compete. The innovations Wal-Mart instituted put it in the position of the most powerful retailer in the world, turning its Operational Innovations into something that ultimately proved to be a category breakthrough. Awareness of the cascading properties of innovation—seeing innovation as fluid—opens up tremendous possibilities for exploration and inspiration.

New inventions that are truly transformational are rare and take decades to discover and capitalize on commercially. But if you use the innovation model to hone your company's true capabilities at all four levels, the results will be far more powerful and financially attractive. What seems like a small idea today may have unimagined possibilities if given the time and resources to mature.

At the GE Global Research Center in Niskayuna, New York, researchers have been working on technology to create a hybrid locomotive for more than ten years. After looking at all the available technology to power such a train, they finally determined that they needed to create their own power source to overcome the challenges of distance and load. This led to the innovation of the sodium battery, and what started out as one idea—a hybrid locomotive—led to something much bigger. Mike Idelchik, vice president of advanced technologies for GE Global Research, explains it this way:

> When our focus turned from the locomotive to the battery, we recognized that the numbers were too small. We couldn't build an economically viable factory just for railroad batteries. So we started to look around and say, "Okay, where does this business technology play?" We

found that these stationary powered applications were relevant in areas such as uninterrupted power supply (UPS) and the telecom industry offering opportunities well beyond trains. Then the battery by itself becomes its own business. Now the locomotive, which drove the project to begin with, will end up being 5 to 10 percent of what we need to make the battery commercially viable. The rest will come from stationary applications and delivery trucks.

This thought process of starting in one place—in this case, filling a need for the railroad industry—and letting it play out or flow to a place that was unimagined is not confined to a GE, Apple, or Wal-Mart. It's a framework for thinking that works in any industry and for any size business. When you open your mind in this way, it becomes less a question of "Can I innovate?" than one of "Where do I start?"

Our advice is to use the model we've outlined in this chapter to help characterize the types of innovation on which you should be focusing your business, then listen to the people who matter most—your customers and consumers. They are the ones who will inspire you, keep you on track, and ultimately determine if your idea is unique, valuable, and worthy of exchange.

CHAPTER 2

Finding Inspiration

Let There Be Light

It's not what you look at; it's what you see.

—HENRY DAVID THOREAU

There's an old joke in the customer service world that goes, "This would be a great job if it weren't for the customers." It's true that customers can be annoying, but as any great innovator will tell you, customers and the insight they provide are *the* most critical drivers of innovation. If what your customers value isn't the basis of your entire agenda, you can waste millions of dollars creating something no one wants to buy—at least not more than once. On the other hand, if your inspiration for innovation at all levels comes from a deep understanding of those you serve, you might end up making history. When VISA envisioned turning debit cards into a profit center for its bank customers, it not only captured a huge share in the financial transactions market, it also helped shape the way most of us shop.

In the last chapter, we talked about the importance of continuous innovation; in this chapter, we'll see where the spark of inspiration for those innovations comes from. To give you a framework to build on, we'll examine five approaches to gaining idea-rich insight and how each can be used to uncover customer wants, needs, and desires that only innovation can fulfill. Along with a description of each approach, we'll tell you how it's been used in the real world to impact the growth and expansion of a company's horizons.

Uncovering insights is just the beginning. Once you've found a nugget of truth, you have to know what to do with it. Where does it fit in the innovation model? Do you have a market breakthrough that will affect next quarter or a big business idea that will transform your company? Knowing where to look for insight, assessing how to use what you learn, and understanding how it fits in your overall business strategy is the next step in bringing continuous innovation to your company. But first you have to know what insight is.

The Ah-Ha Moments

Just as we often think that innovation needs to come from a world-changing idea, we also tend to believe that insight has to hit like a lightning bolt. Typically, though, insight takes the form of an "ah-ha" moment of clarity that unveils a new idea or a new way of looking at something. Think of a kaleidoscope—one of those long tubes filled with brightly colored bits. Each time you turn it, light reflects on the shifting pieces and a beautiful new pattern appears. The same is true of insight. When you shake things up and open your mind to seeing, hearing, and sensing the world around you in a different way, everything changes. Whether the insights you gain are seemingly minimal Marketplace or Operational Innovations or end up being extraordinary transformational or category-changing victories, discoveries are waiting for you, sometimes in the most unexpected places.

Hiding in Plain Sight

While we need insights to inspire a unique way of thinking or doing something, uncovering these gems isn't always easy. Some people—such as Thomas Edison, Henry Ford, Steve Jobs, or Amazon.com's Jeff Bezos—seem to have an intuitive ability that allows them to envision an end result. It's like they can see a light bulb or a virtual bookstore and work through the process of innovation to make it happen. But most of us need a little help. Fortunately, insights are all around if you're open to finding them. To help make this process easier, we've identified five approaches to insight that will yield a wealth of understanding about your customers. The most significant opportunities are where the ah-ha moments lie.

Curiosity

What if? That question has been at the center of innovation insight since early humans picked up a piece of flint and wondered if it might make a useful tool. It's what prompted Sir Isaac Newton to investigate gravity after an apple fell on his head and why the Wright brothers built the machine that gave us wings. It's also why we've been enjoying Campbell's soup for more than a hundred years.

Soups have been around since people first threw leftovers in a pot, and over time, they have evolved from a freshly made meal to a staple in home pantries around the world. How this most ancient of concoctions went from the pot to the cupboard was the doing of a young chemist whose curiosity and passion are still affecting families today.

John Dorrance was fascinated with the science of matter, the branch of the natural sciences dealing with the composition of substances and their properties and reactions. After earning a chemistry degree from Massachusetts Institute of Technology (MIT) and a Ph.D. from the University of Gottingen in Germany, Dorrance returned home ready to put his knowledge to work. A recognized scholar, he was offered prestigious, well-paying teaching jobs, but he really wanted to work for his Uncle Arthur at the Campbell Preserve Company.

To some, it might have seemed an odd choice, but what isn't widely known is that, during his time abroad, young John had fallen in love with the rich soups and sauces of the Europeans. His job gave him the perfect opportunity to combine his fascination with matter and his passion for soup. After several attempts to convince his uncle to hire him, the elder Dorrance finally agreed—on two conditions: John had to settle for a salary of only $7.50 per week, and he had to bring in his own lab equipment.[1]

At the time John joined the company, its primary products were preserves, ketchup, mustards, sauces, and a beefsteak tomato soup. In the late 1890s, soups were popular but found only on the tables of the wealthy in Europe and America. Ready-made soups were available, but while they were inexpensive to produce, they were heavy and thus expensive to ship. This made them extremely impractical for lower- and middle-class families.

As Dorrance thought about the problem, he asked one simple question: what if he could make soups lighter? Would that make them more marketable and affordable? Starting from this concept, he began his experiments. In time, he realized that if he could remove soup's heaviest ingredient, water, he could solve the weight problem. But that created another problem—flavor.

Once water was added back in, the taste was diluted, violating one of the fundamental principles of the food industry. Food has to taste good or no one will buy it! It took three years, but he finally solved the mystery. By making soups in the form of a rich, highly flavored sauce, he could add water to create a warm, delicious soup, and the price was slashed from $0.30 to $0.10 a can. With the lighter packaging, the product was easy to ship, sell, and store, and mealtime preparation was greatly simplified. John's salary was increased to $9.00 a week, and the rest is history.[2]

What is so compelling about the soup tale is both its beginning as a scientific curiosity and its potential to create something that would benefit a large portion of the population. It is this pattern of curiosity and possibility that sets purely scientific inquiry on a path to innovation—and it all started with "what if?"

The same combination that propelled Campbell's soup to superstardom is, more than a hundred years later, setting another creative entrepreneur on a similar path. His journey is to create a new way to keep food, vaccines, medicine, and even a jug of water cool without the need for electricity or fuel of any kind.

His name is Adam Grosser, and he and a group of self-proclaimed geeks at Stanford University have built a fifty-dollar fridge that could change the world.[3] Their inspiration came from a talk Adam heard at a TED conference, a nonprofit dedicated to sharing "ideas worth spreading." The annual event challenges the world's most fascinating thinkers and doers to give the talk of their lives in eighteen minutes.

In 2005, one of those talks gave voice to the critical need to create vaccines that don't require a cool environment to survive. More than a billion and a half people in the world lack electricity and refrigeration, which means they also lack access to important vaccines. Nonprofits are pouring millions into developing these types of vaccines, but tech venture capitalist Grosser has a different idea: don't change the medicine—change the fridge.

Working with a thermodynamics team at Stanford, he built a thermos-sized device that contains a refrigerant that's triggered by heat. When the refrigerant cools, it becomes a powerful cold pack that can turn anything from a jug to a hole in the ground into a twenty-four-hour minifridge. The new "fridge" can be recharged—even over an open fire—in about an hour, and it's small enough to carry around as needed. At roughly $50 a piece (if produced in small quantities) or $25 each (if mass-produced), Grosser's device can potentially bring high-maintenance medicines to people in the developing world or provide the simple pleasure of a cold drink on a hot day. Yesterday's pots of soup in a can and tomorrow's refrigerator in a jug are both amazing breakthroughs sparked by curious minds and the belief that things can not only be different but better. That's the win-win of curiosity-based insight and its journey to true innovation.

When you look at your business, products, and customers, do you only see what and who they are today? Or do you close your eyes and wonder "what if?" Innovation is about seeing beyond the challenges to imagining the solution and being open to the world around us, even if what we see—or hear—is unexpected.

Being Open to New Information and Ideas

Living in a time when there is a constant influx of information, it's easy to become snowed under. Breaking news, research studies, business theories, and customer opinions about virtually everything inundate us; it's overwhelming. Given the deluge of information we live with, it's often easier to close the door on new ideas or input than to stay open to the possibilities they represent, especially if they're things you would rather not hear.

One day a few years ago, Mrs. Peter Darbee was at the gym working out on a treadmill. On this particular day, she was wearing a shirt with the Pacific Gas & Electric (PG&E) logo on it—something a woman walking next to her noticed. "Do you work for that company?" she asked.

"No, my husband gave it to me," Mrs. Darbee said.

"I'd never trust anyone who works for that company! They're crooks, and they take advantage of people," the woman spit back.

Mrs. Darbee was stunned but listened as the woman went on about the terrible experiences she'd had with the company. That night she shared the conversation with her husband, who had just stepped up as the new CEO.

"My wife was embarrassed, and I was shocked," he recalls. "That's not the view I had of who we were as a company, but I swore that night that true or not, we would change the way customers saw us." He made it a priority to find out what customers thought about PG&E and what kind of service they were receiving. Taking a step back, he looked at the utility through their eyes and didn't like what he saw. "I never again wanted anyone to be embarrassed to wear our logo. I told all twenty thousand employees that it was their job—and my job—to make sure it was a symbol we could be proud of."

Since that day Darbee and his team have taken PG&E's public image from an uncaring corporate giant to a winner of the JD Powers Customer Satisfaction Award. They did it by addressing baseline capabilities and focusing on the customer experience. By changing the company focus from being primarily profit-driven to also being customer- and community-centric, PG&E is now recognized as one of California's most respected corporate citizens and an important champion of clean, renewable energy. In fact, it is one of the first major utilities to explore the commercial feasibility of wave power, an energy source with the potential to generate between one and ten terawatts of power. To put this in perspective, just one terawatt could power a billion homes. Successful commercialization of wave power could bring about change that rivals the transformational footprint of the Internet and the affordable automobile. While conquering this force will likely take generations, at the very least PG&E and other companies like it are advancing the possibilities for future visionaries to build on.

In light of the transformation the company has gone through since Mrs. Darbee went to the gym, the question is, have the changes and focus on innovation come about because of that one chance encounter? "In a way, they have," says Darbee. "I'll always be grateful to the woman on the treadmill for opening my eyes when she did. I know she doesn't know it, but she changed the course of our company."

Insights like these shape our priorities, our goals, and our vision of what's possible. Like Darbee, you never know where a conversation, an observation, or a piece of news will lead you. What you can be sure of is that while embracing openness can feel a little like being continually thrown off balance, it's essential to the process of growth and expansion. Being flexible and alert to both reality and possibilities is what enables day-to-day encounters to become commercial points of opportunity.

When Peter Darbee asked his twenty thousand–strong workforce to be the company's eyes and ears with customers, he unleashed a powerful advantage in the marketplace. Having employees who were empowered to observe and listen to customers, no matter what they said, gave the company the insights it needed to create tremendous market change and opportunity. That's a force that's open to everyone.

Necessity

While Peter Darbee allowed himself to be open to the unexpected insight of a chance encounter, you often have to start the conversation yourself. One of the most important questions you can ask when looking for inspiration is, "What do our customers or consumers really *need*?" How can you solve their problems or make their tasks easier? How do you make them feel better about themselves or live a happier life? Fulfilling felt, perceived, or anticipated needs (both practical and emotional) provides the greatest motivator and endless possibilities for innovation. If you can innovate toward fulfilling these needs, you're halfway home. The following modern Cinderella story came from addressing one of women's most basic needs—the need to feel beautiful.[4]

Like so many women, Sara Blakely bought clothes that looked amazing in a magazine or on the hanger, but on her, they magnified every panty line and imperfection. She admits that most of these clothes eventually made their way to the "maybe one day I'll be flawless" section of her closet where they hung unworn.

One day, Sara, who was working as a sales trainer by day and performing as a stand-up comedian at night, wanted to wear a pair of cream-colored pants. She could see that her panty line showed through and was fed up with it. She was not a fan of thongs, and while panty hose would do the trick, she wanted to wear sandals. Having nylon-covered toes just wasn't cool, so in her frustration, she grabbed a pair of scissors and cut the feet off her stockings. Problem solved. "I never thought visible panty lines and uncomfortable thongs would inspire me to be an inventor," she says now. All she knew was that there was nothing out there that was comfortable and functional, so she decided to change that.

After spending her nights at the Georgia Tech Library researching trademarks, patents, and hosiery manufacturers, she set out to patent her idea and create a prototype. Most lawyers thought her idea was so crazy that they later admitted thinking the whole thing was a hoax. Talking with manufacturers didn't go any better. Once again she was sent away, told that her concept made no sense and would never sell. Shortly thereafter, though, she received a call from a mill owner who said he had decided to take on her "crazy" product. When she asked why he'd changed his mind, he said, "I have two daughters." Turns out they didn't think Sara's idea was crazy at all.

The prototype for what she dubbed Spanx took a year to perfect. Once she had a product in hand, she called the buyer at Neiman Marcus and introduced herself over the phone. "I said I had invented a product her customers wouldn't want to live without, and if I could have ten minutes of her time, I'd fly to Dallas," Blakely recalls. "She agreed, and I put the prototype in a ziplock bag from my kitchen, threw it in my good-luck red backpack, and was on a plane. During the meeting, I had no shame. I asked her to follow me to the ladies room where I personally showed her the before and after looks in my cream pants. Three weeks later, Spanx was on the shelves at Neiman Marcus!" In 2006, Target came knocking for Spanx to bring the shapewear revolution to its chain. The result was ASSETS.

Today, the company that was born out of Blakely's frustration has more than a hundred products in its line. "I get my energy and inspiration from inventing and enhancing products that promote comfort and confidence for women," she says. "Customer feedback is one of the key drivers of our business. Spanx Power Panties and High Falutin' Footless were created in response to suggestions from our customers, and there's a lot more to come in the future."

Sara's innovation came from her own experience as a customer, but you can have the same moments of inspiration by stepping into your customers' shoes. Listening to them, asking questions about what's important to their happiness, and seeing what you offer—not just for the task you or your product perform, but also for how it impacts a person's well-being—can open up a world of ideas. In other words, don't just look—see.

One of the best and most well-known companies for going deep into customers' lives for insight is Procter & Gamble (P&G). The company's Living In program places P&G employees in the homes of consumers to observe how people actually live with products and then to find ways to innovate. One lesser-known project took place in an area where people washed laundry by hand. Observers saw that these consumers' laundry detergent, which was developed for machines, didn't dissolve well in washtubs. This wasted soap and made it necessary to rinse clothes several times to get them clean. The process also wasted water and added a considerable amount of time to the chore. None of the women in the regional focus groups had mentioned this problem because, "It's just the way it is." As a result of seeing firsthand how customers used its products, the company was able to come up with a "one-rinse" product that positively impacted customers and the environment.[5]

In essence, what P&G does with its home-visit and Living In programs is akin to detective work—something everyone can do, even if you're not a multinational corporation. Ask yourself, "Where are the clues hidden?" Are they in the home or office where people use your offering? Are they in a grocery store aisle or the streets of a small town? Toyota had its people visiting junkyards to see what kind of damage cars typically experienced. They noticed that most often the sideview mirrors were broken off. This led to the development of the folding mirror. Huggies was born when researchers watched moms interact with their kids while trying to potty train them. Because a Hewlett-Packard product developer took the time to sit in while surgeons operated, the company developed a video monitor that could be suspended on a helmetlike device in front of the physician's eyes during surgery. This replaced a freestanding monitor that people could walk in front of, interrupting the surgeon's view.

When looking for insights based on need, it's important to remember that people often don't know what they need. It's up to you to discover what that unexpressed need might be. People didn't ask for a laundry detergent that was easier to rinse out, a folding side mirror, or a revolutionary new undergarment, but try to take a woman's Spanx away from her and you'd better be ready to run. Find the need and the insight will follow.

Building on an Existing Idea

Have you ever played with those colorful building blocks that children adore and mothers are always finding under the sofa? You start out with one and keep adding a block here and a block there to construct endless creations. Innovation can be that way too. Building on existing ideas is one source of insight that may literally be right under your nose. Maybe you've had an offering that has underperformed or downright flopped. Maybe a product has matured or lost its relevance. If so, you may want to dust it off and take another look. There can be great opportunities buried within old, or even unsuccessful, ideas if you look at them through an innovation lens. That's something Hasbro, one of the largest toy manufacturers in the world, did to transform a $30 million product into a $500 million-plus brand.

The revitalization of the Transformers brand began in 2000 under the leadership of Hasbro's current president and chief executive officer, Brian Goldner. A veteran of advertising agency J. Walter Thompson and Bandai America (makers of Power Rangers), Goldner joined Hasbro when the company was coming off a decade virtually void of innovation. Instead of leading the way, the company was focused on Pokémon imitators and toys licensed from movies. Brands like Transformers and GI Joe "were relegated to an experience that was limited to the playroom floor or the kitchen table," says Goldner. "The history of those brands was much more expansive than we were acknowledging." Buried in that history were huge opportunities for innovation.

Transformers, which joined the Hasbro family in 1984, consists of robots that disguise themselves as vehicles and other technology. The narrative Hasbro created and embedded in the decades-old toy line is about warring factions of valiant Autobots and nefarious Decepticons, who bring their battle to Earth from their home planet of Cybertron. Rich with mythology, the line was a natural for translation to a much larger experience.

To make the leap, the company began looking at the basic premise of the toy—robots in disguise. Recognizing that this view was too narrow and antiquated, Hasbro looked for deeper customer insights. What it learned helped it broaden the original definition of "more than meets the eye" into a stronger moral theme: "you can't judge a book by its cover." This expanded vision of the product has been the inspiration behind the blockbuster *Transformers* movies, igniting new passion for the brand. By 2008, Transformers product sales grew almost fivefold to $484 million from $100 million in 2006. By 2009, they'd passed the $500 million mark.[6]

Hasbro has applied this same strategy of building experience into its other brands, like G.I. Joe and Nerf. As a result, the composition of the business has changed. In 2000, its top eight brands represented around $300 million in revenue; a decade later, that figure had grown to a healthy $2 billion.

"We had to understand that we were not just product stewards," explains Goldner. "We had to embrace that the consumers were already there. We simply had to ignite their imaginations and build around our intellectual property to create a fuller experience. Even our five-year-old customers could frame out what they wanted from us. We just hadn't tapped into that rich source of inspiration to fuel innovation." Because the company dug deeper to let new, relevant insights emerge, it's not just about toys anymore.

Connecting the Dots

This final approach to insight is both a stand-alone tool and an effective last step for the insight producers we've just talked about. Connecting the dots is about linking insights together to create something unique, valuable, and worthy of exchange. It can happen when you suddenly see how a variety of operational processes can be redefined to increase profits or to better serve the customer. It can happen when the point of intersection between a new market you want to develop and a service you've just launched unexpectedly appears. It can occur when you realize that a failure is just the platform you need to create the next generation of products whose time has now come. When the dots are connected, they can lead to amazing business results. When they're not—well, we'll get to that in a minute.

For more than twenty years before the Internet made its way into people's homes, computer scientists were sharing files through what is called peer-to-peer technology. Basically, this just means connecting two computers so they can "talk" to each other by locating addresses and then transferring large amounts of data. It's pretty generic, which made what Swedish entrepreneur Niklas Zennstrom and his Danish buddy Jonas Friis did all the more brilliant. The duo, both of whom are gifted at connecting the dots between technology and consumer needs, gained notoriety in 2000 when they launched an Internet file-sharing service called KaZaA that quickly overtook Napster as the leading venue for swapping free music files. Their success created a wave of controversy and lawsuits from record companies, which eventually led to the sale of the service to Sharman Networks. After the sale was complete, both innovators went underground, and when they resurfaced, it was with a radical new concept: if file sharing worked to find addresses, files, documents, music, movies, or whatever, why can't it find and transfer a stream of data that just happens to be a voice? The answer was—no reason at all.

"When we started Skype, our vision was to create a business that could fundamentally transform the telecommunications industry, and have a big impact, by letting the whole world talk for free," says cofounder Friis. "We wanted to create a great, sustainable communication business."[7]

Within fourteen months of launch, more than 28 million copies of the software that powers Skype on PCs and Linux machines were downloaded. By 2005, the service had 54 million users, making it the fastest-growing Internet service ever. The dots were definitely well connected. Skype was so attractive, in fact, that several suitors showed up—including the eventual winner, eBay, which paid a whopping $2.6 billion for the upstart company.[8]

At the time of the purchase, analysts had trouble seeing the logic of the marriage, or how the dots connected. In fact, the Skype guys admit that at the beginning both parties thought they had little in common. "But when we started talking," Zennstrom says, "we had an 'ah-ha' experience. We went crazy on the whiteboard, mapping out ideas."

At the end of that meeting, they came to the conclusion that Skype could help pull eBay into parts of the world where it was weak, while eBay could extend Skype's relatively limited reach into the United States, providing virtually real shopping through a Skype button on eBay auction pages. eBay believed this Marketplace Innovation would open up a whole new channel for spoken communication among buyers and sellers. And because Zennstrom and Friis were staying on to run Skype, the opportunities for continuing innovation expanded exponentially.

It all made perfect sense—at first. Within four years, Skype grew to include 480 million registered users and posted revenues of $170 million.[9] It was now the most widely adopted international calling system in the world. But despite the continued innovation that brought video and voice together to allow people to talk "in person" online, the direct benefit to eBay was never realized. This was an auction site where the thrill of bidding was one of its biggest draws. People just weren't interested in talking to vendors. Vendors, many of whom were just everyday folks, didn't want to be shopkeepers.

The unhappy marriage ended in 2009, with legal battles over core technology ownership and the eventual sale of 65 percent of the business to private investors for just over $2 billion. eBay's explanation: "It did not mesh well with eBay's core marketplace division."[10] Perhaps another way to say it would be that the dots did not connect well after all.

It is interesting to remember that the initial gut instincts of Skype, eBay, and the analysts were all similar. Each felt that they didn't have enough market crossover to make an obviously strategic marriage. Then the companies convinced themselves otherwise. They forgot to listen to the customers, analysts, or their own people. They listened to the "yes" of their own thinking about possibilities but didn't hear the "no" until it was too late to make it work.

Customers on both the buying and the selling sides of eBay, as well as Wall Street, had trouble understanding the synergy between the two organizations. The risk outweighed the upside, and the proposition failed to please either group. The lesson here is twofold. First, not every ah-ha moment turns out to be great. Risk is inherent in most innovation. Second, there is no substitute for common sense.

The ability to make the leap between what is (insight) and what can be (innovation) is one of the most valuable assets a company can cultivate in its culture and its people, but you have to know the difference between genuine insight and attachment to an idea just because it's sexy, politically correct, or yours. One of the reasons innovation is talked about more than it's actually executed is that many companies are unable to uncover real insight and then properly assess the possibilities. There's a delicate balance between staying open to ideas and managing risk. When you can do both, when you can use all the tools at your disposal to stay in tune with your customers and consumers and correctly determine what's at stake in terms of rewards and sacrifices—that's when the fear of innovation takes a backseat to the possibilities.

CHAPTER 3

Predicting and Managing Risk

Tea Leaf Time

Risk is innovation's middle name.

—BILAL KAAFARANI

One of the greatest challenges a company faces is knowing when to invest time, money, and resources in an idea and when to cut its losses. Risk is part of innovation, and the need to balance risk and reward—to present a picture of financial and leadership success, while betting on an unknown—is a reality CEOs have to face every day.

Adding to the pressure, boards, shareholders, and the press are constantly evaluating a leader's viability based on "snapshots" that often have nothing to do with the big picture. No wonder more than a few leaders shy away from innovation. In fact, one Fortune 100 CEO we know told the company's head of innovation, "I'll only invest in new product research if it has a

100 percent chance of being commercially viable." Ridiculous as that expectation was, it helps underscore the tremendous pressure today's leaders feel to avoid failure. Innovation is never easy or foolproof. In fact, in its simplest form, it's as much about risk management as it is about creation.

When she was growing up, Jane's father used to say, "Life is a series of trade-offs. Whenever you get something, remember you traded something to get it. Just make sure you know what you've traded for the exchange." That's good advice for life in general, but it's also relevant to innovation. Even if you minimize risk, as our cautious CEO tried to do, you may be trading off the chance for a huge upside. With innovation, the bigger the risk, the greater the upside. Although nothing else about innovation is guaranteed, that you can count on. Risk is part of the game, and while risk will never be eliminated, there are ways to keep it within the bounds of acceptability.

Risk and the Four Levels

Just as people have individual talents and tolerances, the four levels of innovation also have distinct capabilities and risk profiles. Just as you need to understand how to work with people, you also need to understand how to work with distinct innovation levels to achieve the best outcomes. When it comes to risk and the four levels, there's a simple rule of thumb that works every time: the more known factors there are (like market size, technology, and costs) and the more direct control you have over the outcome of these factors, the lower the risk. Conversely, the less you know, the greater the risk. Knowing what your risk level is going in is not only helpful with planning and funding, it also helps you set expectations that are realistic—especially with something as unpredictable as Transformational Innovation.

Transformational-Level Risk

Transformational Innovation is all about risk. Typically born out of invention or curiosity about whether something is possible, in the beginning it's not much more than an idea you believe has value. You're not sure what the product is, who your customer might be, or when/if it will ever make money. But something about it won't let you go. That's the reality of Transformational Innovation.

Why then, in today's risk-averse society, would anyone want to take a chance on Transformational Innovation? For starters, if no one did, it would mean that society as we know it would stand still. Our world is constantly evolving, and what we want and need evolves too. It would also mean that future generations would be in the same bind that many of us are in right now—stuck in stagnant or negative growth. We understand that not every company is capable of Transformational Innovation, but we need those who are willing to take risks and invest in long-term possibilities. If you are one of the visionaries who is up for the challenge, then there are a few risk-related things you need to know.

First of all, Transformational Innovation can't survive traditional corporate metrics. With a few notable exceptions such as Apple, where Steve Jobs still operates from the entrepreneurial spirit and control of a small start-up, the corporate environment spells death to Transformational Innovation. This type of innovation needs room to explore possibilities without the demand for short-term results. Most companies don't have this freedom built into their funding process or pipeline strategy, but by its very nature, the high-risk orientation of something that is truly transformational requires a distinct set of processes that incubate and cultivate possibilities in a nurturing way. Doing it any other way would be like taking a bird's egg out of a nest and dropping it from an airplane to see if it could fly—not something any of us would do.

You would first want to keep the egg warm and then, once the chick hatched, ensure that nothing scary ate it—like finance. Once the little creature matured to a level of self-sufficiency, then and only then would you push it out of the nest to see if it could fly. Otherwise, the odds would not be worth taking.

The key here is to provide an incubator environment that allows you to take calculated risks. Without it, the unpredictability and long-term horizon for commercial adoption are untenable. It took decades for the Internet to become commercially viable. Not only did the technology, product ideas, and customer sets have to be developed, there was also the market readiness factor. It often takes a long time for truly transformational products or services to take hold and be socially adopted. True success happens when it all comes together. When you're willing to take the risk, the upside is, well, transformational.

Think about the financial success of Google, Amazon, and eBay. Those three companies alone equal a market capital of well over $200 billion—yes, $200 billion. And none of them would exist without the Transformational Innovation of the Internet. Without this high-risk/high-reward segment of innovation, many of the things we take for granted—like charge cards, cars, airplanes, electricity, penicillin, vaccines, and someday soon, mobile payments—wouldn't exist.

Western Union is a company that's placing a huge investment bet on its mobile payments business. Christina Gold, the company's CEO, shared her views on this potentially Transformational Innovation shortly before she announced her retirement.

"Mobile payments is an as-yet-undefined business, but someone will define it, and when they do, it will change the world," explained Gold. "We haven't done it yet, but we've made strides in Africa, where millions of people have limited access to banking and bill-paying services. Western Union's vision is to give people the ability to transfer money and pay for physical goods and services using tap-and-pay on mobile devices. With this new technology, users would be able to remit money to another person anywhere in the world by knowing only his or her mobile phone number. On the surface, this might seem easy to do, but in truth, it's very complex."

Successful mobile money service offerings are normally deployed on a single-country basis. Within that country, three service providers work together in a single "mobile finance ecosystem." This system combines mobile network operators with well-known consumer brands and large mobile subscriber bases; financial institutions with the legal and regulatory authority to store and hold money; and mobile market providers (often called m-wallet, or m-banking, markets) capable of managing account interaction between the consumer handset, the wireless network, and the financial institution. It's anything but easy, but the one who figures out how to simplify the network and make it global will win big. Western Union is connecting into this ecosystem, providing money-transfer capability under a global brand with proven speed and reliability. It's a complicated undertaking that requires certifying vendors and then providing the technical expertise to pull it all together.

"I ask myself all the time, 'Are we the ones to do this?'" said Gold. "There is probably no other company in the world that has the expertise in payments that we do or the global footprint we do. We also understand the unique issues of money transfer in the most remote areas of the world. While it's a 'big bet' investment, it's something we felt we couldn't pass on. I say 'we,' but ultimately, I have to be the one to provide the needed investment and protection to develop this business. Because the risk/reward scenario is so long term, none of our geography heads could afford to put this funding ahead of innovation that will pay off in the next three to twelve months. Without unique support, this project would never even have the chance to succeed. It's high risk, but if it succeeds, it could change the way people handle money all over the world."

That being the case, it's not too early for you to be thinking about how this will affect your business and where you might be able to innovate at the next level. Riding on the coattails of

Transformational Innovation has built empires. You just need to be open to ideas and willing to take the leap.

Category-Level Risk

While Transformational Innovation is almost all risk, Category Innovation is an equal mix of risk and opportunity. Although stemming from successful Transformational Innovations like the light bulb, the Internet, or mobile payments, the application or the customer segment addressed by Category Innovation is new. By its very nature, this type of innovation is entirely incremental to current revenue streams. It's true that the upside is unpredictable, but if it works, it can be as big as the iPhone.

The reason for this is that with Category Innovation, there are always factors that can't be predicted or defined. Either the technology is a risk or the market has never been addressed and can't be quantified. Then there's the cost of delivery. It's a best guess until it hits production or service launch. Each project has its own variables, making it hard to pin down in the initial stages. That's why so many leaders delay their decision to move forward until they have better or more reliable information. This tendency to delay until hard facts are available can be dangerous though. The more you try to force a new technology or developing market segment into a quantifiable risk profile early on, the more fear you'll instill in the very people who know the most about why this is or isn't a good business risk.

Without a doubt, Category Innovation tests leadership courage, but without some failures, there can be no big successes. The trick is to assess what you do know and the credibility of those involved. Then determine how much risk the unanswered questions represent. Once you've done that, you can marry the risk level to the state of your business. Do you have room for the investment to fail? Can you afford *not* to move forward? Or perhaps the question is, what must be done to further mitigate the risk before plunging ahead?

Ultimately, Category Innovation is about building your confidence in making at least some decisions based on business instincts and belief—even if it means your head could be on the chopping block. There's an old adage that proves true here, "If you can't stand the heat, get out of the kitchen." To fuel the growth engine, today's leaders have to create a climate of possibility, not fear. Make no mistake: an organization based on fear will *never* deliver sustainable innovation and growth.

Today, Ford is riding high as an effectively innovative organization, but it wasn't always that way. No one remembers that more painfully and honestly than Bill Ford. When the company was in the tightening vise of financial difficulty, the hybrid car was at a critical stage of development. At the same time, sales were in the tank, products weren't viewed to be as trustworthy as Japanese- or German-built alternatives, and the company was suffering from a lack of innovation success left over from the previous decade. As a result, the environment was one of greater and greater levels of fear and short-term thinking. Everyone was looking for a quick fix.

Then, as now, cost cutting was the name of the game, and the word *silos* had taken on a whole new meaning. Engineering was pointing the finger at marketing; marketing was pointing the finger at sales; the dealerships were pointing the finger at headquarters; and manufacturing was just plain discouraged. As Bill tells it, most innovation got caught in the mire of what he calls "the clay layer." This is the barrier between the people who really make things happen and the leaders who can actually make decisions to remove barriers and take action.

Bill decided that if there was one thing he would do while leading Ford, it would be to sponsor the hybrid, saving it from demise by the clay layer. Because it was a new technology paired with an existing technology and addressed a market whose size wasn't reliably definable, he had to place a big bet and stick to his guns. In light of the trouble most carmakers found themselves in during the economic downturn, it's now clear that this was a risk Ford had no choice but to take.

Before we move on, it's important to note that we are not suggesting in any way that you should routinely place big bets on the unknown without quantifying factors that can help you anticipate the projected upside and understand the dreaded downside. As Bill Ford says, "I don't think risk taking is generally the way to go. We've had risk-taking leaders who put half-baked ideas forward, and they weren't answering the questions customers were asking. They were innovating through the rear-view mirror.

"Innovation is about identifying great ideas, understanding what customers really want and need, and knowing what it will take to deliver in the marketplace. Our greatest capability for identifying and actually commercializing these new ideas has come from real teamwork between engineering, product development, and marketing. That's the partnership that minimizes our risk by answering more questions than we ever asked before and collaborating on what the right projections are."

We'll talk more about how to make qualified risk assessments later in the chapter. For now, just know that by making risk assessment a pivotal part of your innovation thinking, you can better protect the investments that have a chance to make it and end those that don't—before they break the bank.

Marketplace-Level Risk

When you step out into the world of Marketplace Innovation, you're moving into a zone where risk is fairly controllable. That's because this type of innovation is more about broadening and reviving your customer base than it is about originating one. The same is true of the product or technology on which your Marketplace Innovation is based. You're usually updating or customizing something that already exists rather than creating something new. When you do this, there's risk, but it's lower because you can build on technology or design investments you've already made and on feedback from customers you understand fairly well. Even when a Marketplace Innovation is completely new (in other words, not based on previous iterations), the risk is lower than it is with Category or Transformational Innovation, because the cost is lower.

Marketplace Innovations are less risky from a time perspective as well. They usually happen quickly and require fewer resources; therefore, the risk is automatically lowered. That's good news if you're looking for incremental growth or replacement revenue that would otherwise be lost to competitors if you don't keep up. This is the level where you weigh the risk of not innovating against the advantages of keeping your company and offerings fresh. If a product has lost its relevance to business or society, or if it becomes stagnant, you don't really have a choice. It's literally innovate or languish.

For years, the growth of bagels and Kraft's Philadelphia Cream Cheese was synergistic. But as the growth of the bagel slowed down, so too did Philly's. "We weren't growing. In fact, we were in danger of shrinking," recalls Bilal, who was working for Kraft at the time. "We had to find another outlet to stimulate purchases and invent new occasions for use.

"So I started by looking at what we knew: bagel sales were stagnant. This was due, in part, to the fact that heart-health issues were making the news almost daily, and people were more cautious about the fat content they were taking in. We also knew that people used Philly mostly at breakfast. Since we clearly didn't want cream cheese to be a one-use or one-timeslot product, that's where we had to start.

"The question we began with was, what other Philly carriers were out there? Chips, bread, breadsticks, crackers, vegetables, fruits? What did people put creamy food on? Once we had that answer, we asked if people were satisfied with what they put on these carriers. Was there a *reason* for another product? Even though we wanted the answer to be yes, we didn't know for sure, so we did market research to find out. We also looked at our timeslot—breakfast. What carrier dominated breakfast and could create synergistic opportunities for cream cheese?"

The answer was toast.

It was on nearly every breakfast table, and Philly had a better health profile than butter, the most common spread. With this insight in hand, innovation followed. Kraft developed new science to turn the hard, thick, traditional cream cheese into a spreadable delight that not only found its way onto the breakfast table, but also expanded to the dessert table, the tailgate party, and even the spoon for a late-night snack in flavors that continue to evolve. Originally dubbed Philly for Toast, it was later renamed what most of us are familiar with today—Whipped Philly.

This story, which is typical of many Marketplace Innovations, took an insight about a problem, married it to a solution, and then leveraged the hell out of it. The core audience was broadened, but it also replaced the consumers who were shying away from bagels. The product was reformulated, but the expense was contained. This is because the initial development costs were still being maximized, and the business was revitalized by creating a new platform on which to build.

Marketplace Innovations like this one should be a staple of any business. Whether it's a product, a service, or a never-before-tried marketing and sales innovation, such projects excite people and help develop an innovation mind-set. It doesn't hurt that Marketplace Innovations, when done right, are cost-effective, incremental, and highly predictable. Best of all, they can often be produced in time for next quarter's analyst meeting. Is there risk? Sure, but like our next type of innovation, the upside can be well worth it.

Operational-Level Risk

If we were to catalog innovation over the past one hundred years, we have no doubt that a great many achievements would fall into the operational category. Operational Innovation is the easiest to define and can be managed more effectively than the other types. There are several reasons for this. First of all, Operational Innovation is internally focused—meaning it is concerned with efficiency, effectiveness, sustained quality, and cost value to the company—so you have more control over all the elements. Also, it's more predictable (if I do this, that will happen). Finally, the investment it requires can be more easily tied to outcome (if I spend this, my return is projected to be that). But even though Operational Innovation is less risky on the surface, don't be fooled into thinking it's a no-brainer. True Operational Innovation is about tackling big questions about how your company is run and how you can serve customers better. That often means making changes to the status quo or committing to investments in people and technology, even when everyone else is holding back.

The years since 2007 have been riddled with uncertainty, rising costs, and economic downturn for many airlines. One company, though, has been enjoying particularly good times despite the challenges. In the past decade, Dubai-based Emirates Airlines has grown from a regional carrier to one of the top three international airlines. Central to its success is an innovative, French-built jetliner, the Airbus A380. Operating at a 12 percent lower cost than rival Boeing's newest 747, it can carry up to five hundred passengers, significantly reducing the expense per head. What's more, its long-range capability allows the company to take advantage of its home base in Dubai to capture intercontinental traffic from North America to Asia and from Europe to Asia and Australia.[1]

The savings and reach have helped Emirates to undercut the fares of established rivals like Lufthansa, Air France-KLM, and Singapore Airlines, while still making money. Emirates reported net income of $964 million through March 2010. Then it turned around and ordered thirty-two more A380s valued at $11 billion, giving the company more superjumbos than any other carrier. To put this growth in perspective, it took Lufthansa forty years to get thirty 747s in the air.[2]

Although there is risk in such ambitious operational investment, innovations like these can have a profound impact on a business today and can help redefine possibilities for the future. With new technology making it feasible for any two points on the globe to be connected with just one stop, the carrier that can make the leap will have tremendous advantages. The smart company looks ahead. In fact, when it comes to Operational Innovation, the greater risk is doing nothing at all.

This is the type of innovation that needs to be happening in every business 24/7. It's the underpinning that allows the innovation engine to run well. Having said that, we also need to add a word of caution. While you need Operational Innovation to foster growth, you need Marketplace, Category, or Transformational Innovation by its side to drive it. Emirates' operational breakthroughs are supported by Marketplace Innovations that attract customers to fill up the superjumbo fleet. In addition to the flatbed seats other airlines offer only in first class, the A380s have showers and digital consoles that keep people connected to the world flying by beneath them. This free flow of innovation from one level to another ensures that the airline's innovations are maximized; the Marketplace Innovations attract customers and keep them coming back, and the Operational Innovations make sure there are enough seats to meet the demand. This win-win synergy minimizes risk and keeps the company innovating on multiple levels—something every business needs to do. In fact, no business can truly say it's dedicated to innovation-driven growth unless it is engaged at multiple levels. Knowing the (individual and combined) risks and rewards at each level helps you balance the innovation pipeline and makes it easier to make critical decisions.

To Fund or Not to Fund—
That Is the Question

Whether it's a risky proposition like Transformational or Category Innovation, or something more predictable in the arena of Marketplace or Operational Innovation, funding is always an issue. Too often, when you look at the profit-and-loss statement, there's no room for risk, especially at the higher levels. That's why funding innovation often needs to be done outside a company's day-to-day operations. If the return is more than a year off, the money's not going to be there unless innovation has an advocate with power over the purse strings. General Electric is one company that recognizes these funding challenges and has developed a way to ensure that money is available when the risk/reward profile uncovers a potential winner. Over the course of writing this book, we had the opportunity to participate in GE innovation review sessions that directly addressed funding and how to decide which ideas lived or died.

These unique sessions give people two to four levels below Jeffrey Immelt, GE's chairman and CEO, the opportunity to present a quick overview of their transformational or category ideas directly to him. This is done without any supervision from the leader of their global business unit or division. The snapshots these individuals present include the potential customer base, their best guess of the market potential (based on analytics, insights, and intuition), estimated pricing and costs, and any barriers to entry.

After each presentation, Immelt drills down on areas of potential risk and opportunity before deciding if a project is worthy of special funding and support. Those that are blessed move forward under the protective umbrella of Immelt and the heads of marketing and technology.

We observed that when a transformational project came up, most of the focus was on how the possibility could be cultivated to a stage where the risk could be assessed. When the project was a Category Innovation, the focus was on the market and what the potential derailers might be. This is an excellent perspective to take. If the upside isn't great enough to imagine the possibilities and want to make those possibilities a reality, then it probably isn't a risk you want to take. On the other hand, if the possibilities are so exciting that you want to ensure they have a shot at succeeding, it's worth going to the next level. In time, there will be enough data to assess the risk of funding the project through to commercialization.

What GE is doing with its assessment process is exactly what Hasbro's CEO, Brian Goldner, refers to when he suggests failing early and often versus late and expensively. That's why Goldner also recommends what he calls "the martini glass method of funding."

According to him, "Picture a martini glass. It's at the widest point where you want to gather the most ideas and determine if they're really worth pursuing. By identifying winners and losers early in the process (at the widest part of the glass), you can better manage what breakthrough concepts have an actual chance of moving forward, and those are the ones that get funded. This approach saves time and money and is a disciplined way to determine products you put in the pipeline, because as you travel toward the bottom, narrower part of the martini glass, the costs grow exponentially."

If you apply this thinking to the levels of innovation, the wide mouth of the glass represents the Marketplace and Operational Innovation levels that are part and parcel of your lower-risk investments. Innovation at this widest part of the martini glass can be expected to provide financial returns in the short term, say three to twelve months. Next is the narrowing bowl of the glass, which defines investments for Category Innovation that are three to five years out. Last is the bottom of the bowl—a narrow, but still fundamental, part of the glass—which defines Transformational Innovation investments. These need incubating, protection, and funding that is not tied to traditional corporate metrics. When you look at funding in this way, by level and timeline, it makes it easier to decide where your money should go.

We're not done yet, though. To further assess risk, we're adding another dimension that takes us deeper into places you may not want to go and asks questions you may not want to answer. But if you do, what's waiting on the other side is sweet indeed.

CHAPTER 4

Innovation
That Performs

The Sweet Spot

I don't want to invent anything that won't sell.

—THOMAS EDISON

When Martin Glenn joined Birds Eye in 2006, it was probably because he loved a challenge. Faced with rising costs from a bad crop of peas, expensive cooking oils, and soaring milk prices that cut into its creamed spinach profits, the food manufacturer needed to make some serious changes. In his first months as CEO, Glenn went through the usual exercises of examining costs and looking for ways to extend lines and open up new markets. But no matter where he looked, he kept coming back to one thing—fish.

The British-based company's audience is serious about its fish fingers. Research showed that customers were happy with the cod fingers Birds Eye had given them for fifty years, and they weren't about to change. Glenn discovered, however, that another fish—Alaskan pollock—was more plentiful than cod and reproduced much more quickly. Switching would not only save the company money, but it would be better for the environment. It made both business and scientific sense, and it also aligned with research on social concerns. What was missing was buy-in from consumers who were not only perfectly happy with what they had but had expressed unwillingness to change.

The company was faced with the perception that cod was a superior fish. This was partly due to familiarity. People don't like to risk change if they're happy with what they have. Also, the public had been told for years that cod was the best. There was no forcing the issue, people believed what they believed, and that's what Birds Eye had to change. To that end, the company embarked on advertising and public relations campaigns that touted the environmental sustainability and health benefits of *Alaskan* pollock. This wasn't just any old fish, but a special fish from the icy, fresh waters of a special place. Within months, consumers were engaged and confident that they were getting something better than ordinary cod. This focus on cultural adoption took the company from being 5 percent in the red to 5 percent in the black, a 10 percent swing in just one year.[1]

What Birds Eye and Glenn did wasn't miraculous; it was calculated. Faced with a business challenge, they turned to innovation for the solution, and when they found it, they made sure that customers were on board. In other words, they had all their bases covered, lowering risk and greatly improving the probability of incremental growth when they needed it most. In this final chapter of Part 1, we're going to introduce you to a framework that guides you through a set of checks and balances to make sure your innovation projects have the best chance for life in the marketplace. Like the concept of the four levels, it is simplicity itself—just three small words—but what power they hold.

The Three Ws

When most people see three Ws these days, they automatically think of the World Wide Web. From now on though, whenever you see these letters, we want you to think innovation—or more precisely, *who*, *what*, and *why*. These three words can do more to change the way you look at innovation risk than anything you've ever encountered before.

Imagine if you will, three circles, each representing a different facet of innovation. The first holds customers, or those *who* will buy your offering. The second encompasses *what* you are developing—your products or services and everything needed to deliver them, whether it's science, technology, process, or capabilities. The third circle is the *why*: why does the innovation you're considering make business sense? It's here that you think through costs, resources, timelines, and the potential upside to decide for (or against) pursuing the innovation. The more you know about each circle, the more you lower risk and increase reward.

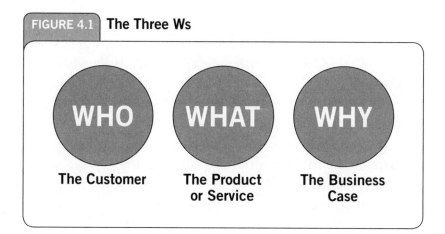

FIGURE 4.1 The Three Ws

WHO — The Customer
WHAT — The Product or Service
WHY — The Business Case

It's elegantly simple. In fact, most companies already have the capabilities to use this concept. They just don't bring all the elements together. Instead, they treat these elements as separate entities through marketing, research and development, engineering, and finance. Not only does this split vision add to the risk of innovation, it can sometimes actually kill it. What you're looking for isn't separate accountability, but synergistic alignment. By looking at the three circles together and knowing that each supports and flows into the others, you get a truer picture of the risk it will take to give an innovation life. In other words, instead of a snapshot you get a veritable 3D movie on which to base decisions. When the three circles align so that they actually intersect, it takes you to that sweet spot we mentioned in Chapter 3, the place where innovation has the greatest chance for success.

We'll explain this in more detail after we talk about the individual circles, but first, there are two things to note in looking at this alignment. First is the matter of equality. Throughout this book, we say that the customer is *the* critical ingredient in innovation success. That's true as a general principle, but when it comes to assessing risk, no one circle is more important than the other. Alignment and intersection are what we're looking for. This means each W holds equal weight.

The second thing to note is that it doesn't matter where you begin the process of alignment. It depends on what type of innovation you're working on—that's why it's important to know going in if it's operational, marketplace, category, or transformational. If it's a Marketplace or Operational Innovation, you'll have access to insight about your customers, who they are, and what they value. So starting there makes sense. For Category and Transformational Innovation, you might not know who your customers are for a long time, so waiting for these answers will only sidetrack your progress. With these two types of innovation, the starting point is almost always

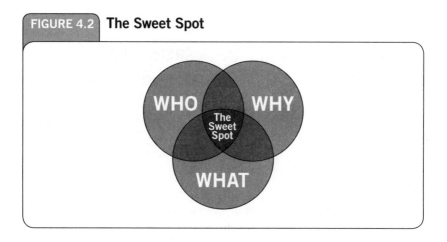

FIGURE 4.2 The Sweet Spot

curiosity involving science, technology, or some unique way of doing things.

Regardless of where you start, you need to know what each circle encompasses. To help you with this, we've developed a set of questions for each area, with some prompts to make sure you don't leave out anything important. Complete as many as you can and put a question mark next to those you can't. At the end of this section, we'll tie it all together and show beyond a shadow of a doubt how paying attention to the three Ws can turn even the worst of times into something to celebrate.

The Who

Every innovation needs someone to buy it. It's as simple as that. Without knowing *who* that person or company is, you can't project the market, finish development, or apply metrics. This is where the understanding and insight we talked about in Chapter 2 comes into play. Use all your customer insight resources to answer the questions in Table 4.1. Also, since this tool is meant to be a guide and not a rulebook, add any questions that are relevant to your customers, consumers, or company that we may have left out. What's important is to know as much as possible about *who* in order to determine risk.

TABLE 4.1 **Who**

WHO QUESTIONS	REMINDERS
Who *exactly* are your customers?	Support your answer with analytics, insight, and intuition.
What are the demographics, ethnographics, and psychographics?	Define your business's size, geography, profit margin, growth objectives, credibility, synergies, adjacencies, and ability to adapt to change.
What are your customers' current buying habits?	Define how habits might impact your innovation, both positively or negatively.
What kind of quality are customers expecting?	Be sure to define whether customers' expectations are based on what is currently possible/accepted or on what they *really* want.
How do customers define and experience value?	Look at all dimensions of value: physical, intellectual, emotional, and spiritual. Identify what your customers currently value and how your innovation will increase value.
What would satisfy customers, what would delight them, and what would surprise them?	Consider what customers currently expect and what they think is impossible to get.
How easily will customers understand the significance of your innovation?	This speaks directly to rate of adoption. An innovation that is easy to understand and has intuitive value has a faster rate of adoption.
What problem does the innovation solve, or what opportunity does it create?	Clearly define exactly what the innovation will bring to the customer—how will it impact his or her life?

continued

WHO QUESTIONS	REMINDERS
What are the dissatisfiers or limitations of current competitive offerings or previous iterations?	Learn from others' mistakes!
What are the relevant touch points in the customer experience? Where are the gaps?	Look at everything: packaging, ease of purchase, service levels, ease of use, storage, disposal, and so on. In the case of services, look at wait time, deliverables, and follow-up.
What was the adoption rate of comparable innovations in the past (if available)?	Determine what hindered or aided innovations similar to the one you're proposing. If it's as unfamiliar as the Internet was, expect a long adoption rate. Something people recognize—like a mobile device—could take off like the iPhone!

Once you have answered as many of the questions as possible, you can move on to the next circle. If you weren't able to answer all the who questions, don't worry. It simply means you either need to feel confident enough to take the risk or should wait until you can, to further minimize the risk.

The What

This circle is the innovation itself. It covers what it will take to deliver the product or service to make sure it really works. Sometimes that means inventing a new science or technology or creating an innovative process, as Henry Ford did when he came up with the first affordable automobile or as Kraft did when it created spreadable cream cheese. In other cases, it might mean a new design such as the one Sara Blakely came up with for Spanx. It's also possible that it's not the product or the technology but regulations or laws that you need to define in order to reduce risk. Whatever the *what* is, this is the place to find out where you stand.

TABLE 4.2 **What**	
WHAT QUESTIONS	**REMINDERS**
Is it an existing product or a newly invented technology, science, or service?	Do your homework to make sure you fully understand what's out there and where in the continuum you fit between modification and leading or bleeding edge.
What are the unique advantages?	Be brutally honest about what truly differentiates your product.
Is it patentable, or is it a trade secret?	Understand what protection you actually have and decide whether it is enough to give you competitive lead time.
What is the time horizon—one year, three years, or five or more years?	Think only in terms of timing you know you can deliver on.
What regulatory or compliance measures are required?	How much control will you have over getting the necessary approvals? Have you factored that into your timing projections?
In combination with consumer needs and business insights, does it shift society? Create new categories? Transition a current technology?	Know what impact the product will have if the market and business cases line up to support the product development. The bigger the impact, the more palatable the risk may be.

continued

WHAT QUESTIONS	REMINDERS
Are you applying diverse thinking to the proposition?	How many different types of people have you gotten input from? Is the input or feedback consistent, regardless of diverse backgrounds and perspectives?
Does your business have the patience to wait on the needed development time?	Do you have the resources and leadership buy-in needed to get the idea over the fence to commercial development?

Just as with the *who* circle, answer as many questions as you can, filling in the blanks as you progress. For short-term innovations, all of these questions should be relatively easy to answer. With projects that require new inventions, the timeline will be longer. As it gets closer to completion and is more definable, you should be able to gather more risk-lowering information. Remember GE's battery innovation for railroads? When the company started out, it was looking for a single-industry solution, but as the research progressed workers were able to see adjacent applications, which helped broaden the definition of the *who*. With a larger commercial transportation market to sell to, the risk was automatically reduced—good news for our next circle.

The Why

Our final circle is the business case, or *why* it does or doesn't make business sense to undertake an innovation. It may seem to be a no-brainer that a company would know this before going ahead with a project, but we've seen too many fail at innovation because they didn't define the business case in realistic terms. Wanting, needing, or knowing you should be innovating is not a sound reason to undertake a project. You need to know *why* it makes sense financially, competitively, and strategically in order to know whether it's worth the risk.

TABLE 4.3 Why

WHY QUESTIONS	REMINDERS
What is the market potential one, three, five, and ten years out?	Think in terms of both minimum and maximum, but plan for minimum.
Who are and will be your competitors?	Can you give in-depth information about the current competitive land-scape, as well as project others' plans for the future?
Are you offering something unique and differentiated?	How unique is your offering, and what does that mean relative to pricing, access, and so on.
How do you make money (margins, growth, cost of goods, return on investment)?	What are the costs of production, and what pricing will the market support? Make sure you have all the details about the needed supply chain, distribution mechanisms, and sales projections to ensure that profitability is possible.
What defines a commercial win?	Understand what measures will indicate success.
Do you have brands that can carry you through?	Know the brand power, or lack of brand power, you have to leverage.
How do you defend the business?	What barriers to entry are there for competitors? Do you know what will allow you to win in the long term?
What is your business plan or strategy?	Have you taken the time to fully define all aspects of the business and to set a strategy to deliver the business case profitably?

With the questions for all three circles answered, you can now see where the pitfalls lie. As we said before, the more questions left unanswered, the greater the risk; the more time you take to fill in the blanks and bring the circles into alignment, the more likely your success. Earlier we talked about Birds Eye.

When the company embarked on its innovation of fish fingers, it had two of the three circles aligned—a product that met market needs (if not expectations) and a business case that improved profitability. What was missing was the customer, so the company took the necessary steps to bring that third circle into alignment. Birds Eye could have launched its new product with sexy new packaging and fanfare, banking on customers to play along. With this strategy, the pushback from customers could have been considerable. But by marrying its knowledge about its customers with the broader worldview of environmental responsibility, Birds Eye was able to turn a potential loser into a clear winner.

It's important to note that at one time the original cod-based product was very successful and the three Ws were aligned. But costs rise, markets fluctuate, and customers evolve. When a business case drives innovation, you have to be sure you know exactly how you're going to bring all three circles into alignment to minimize risk. This is especially true at the marketplace and operational levels, where companies tend to think short term and cut corners hoping for quick returns.

This approach of looking at the three circles and making sure that all the questions are answered works no matter which circle you're starting from or what level of innovation you're attempting. Sometimes it's a customer insight that drives innovation, as we saw with Spanx, or a technological or scientific breakthrough like Skype or the fuel-free fridge. Whichever circle leads the way, finding the sweet spot where they all intersect is the essence of creating innovations that work. We can't ask for more than that.

Bringing It Home

In discussing innovation performance, we wanted to illustrate how all the components come together, not just for one company, but for an entire industry over the span of a century. Since Bilal spent more than a decade working with the product we'll be talking about, we thought it would be a good fit.

To start our adventure, let's visit a restaurant in upstate New York. No reservations required. As the story unfolds, we'll interject comments to tie the lesson back to everything we've talked about in Part 1 so you can more easily apply the points to your own business. Keep in mind that although this story is about a consumer product, the same principles apply equally to business-to-business interactions. As in all things to do with innovation, the customer and consumer lead the way.

A Chip Off the Old Block

In the summer of 1853, a young man named George Crum was working as a chef at the elegant Moon Lake Lodge resort in Saratoga Springs, New York. One of the favorite menu items was a French-style potato cut lengthwise, lightly fried, and eaten with a fork. As the story goes, Crum became irritated when a customer sent his fried potatoes back to the kitchen—not once, but twice—complaining that they were cut too thick. Crum, who by all accounts was a temperamental and sarcastic man, reacted by slicing the potatoes in small, paper-thin rounds, then frying them to a crisp in grease. Hoping to further exact revenge on the insult to his cooking, he smothered the mess in salt. But the smirk fell off his face as he watched the guest and his companions devour the concoction. They loved it! In fact, so many others did as well that they began asking for them, and Crum's "Saratoga chips" became one of the lodge's most popular items, proving once again that if you listen and keep an open mind, ideas for innovation are all around you.

Though Crum may not have thought of his chips as an innovation, they were, in fact, the beginning of a budding new industry and a nice business for him. A few years after the picky customer incident, Crum opened his own restaurant, and despite long lines because of his policy of not taking reservations, people still waited to taste his chips. Like Ben Franklin with his lightning rod, however, inventor/chef Crum never patented or tried to widely distribute his potato chips. Other restaurants soon began offering the freshly made chips. As their popularity grew, they caught the eye of a number of aspiring snack-food entrepreneurs, and the innovation cascade began.

One such entrepreneur was William Tappendon, a businessman from Cleveland, Ohio, who began making potato chips in 1895, first in his kitchen and later in a makeshift factory in his barn. After peeling and slicing the potatoes by hand, he fried them in large kettles, then loaded them in tins and took them to grocery stores.[2] There the snacks were sold in bulk from barrels or out of glass display cases and taken home in paper bags. This expansion of the chip from a restaurant treat to a take-home delight moved the innovation into an adjacent category (from food service to grocery). Tappendon knew customers loved the product, that he had the means to make it, and that he could make a profit. This was the first sign that the potato chip had the potential to move into the sweet spot.

Thinking Outside the Barrel

As time went on, potato chips gained in popularity, and innovations like the mechanical potato peeler and the automatic fryer (both Operational Innovations) made it possible to increase production to the point that it became profitable for smaller regional producers. Over the next two decades, potato chip factories popped up from Ohio south to Texas and east to Massachusetts and Pennsylvania. All of them were regional successes, but each faced common problems—freshness and breakage.

One of the reasons the chips were so well loved in restaurants was their crisp, fresh taste when they came straight from the fryer to the table. When prepared ahead, transported, and stored in grocery store barrels and bins, some of the chips broke. In a matter of days, the taste and texture also began to change.

Even after frying, potatoes retain moisture, and oil turns rancid when it's exposed to oxygen. Chips at the bottom of the barrel were often soggy and stale, and the shelf life was virtually nil.

While all companies understood both of these problems, it was a West Coast entrepreneur named Laura Scudder who came up with the solution. Scudder had a curious mind and a thirst for knowledge. Originally a nurse in Philadelphia, she later became an attorney in Ukiah, California, and then founded her food company after moving to Monterey. Her first product was potato chips, which she shipped in barrels or tins like everyone else. She did well, but like others before her, freshness and breakage were issues. Of all the challenges, these were the ones no one had solved. They were holding back sales, moving the business case and technology circles further away from the customer. What was needed was an Operational Innovation. Oil and air were the problems, but while most companies tried to attack the enemy in the kitchen, Laura took the battle to the packing plant.

Each night she sent her female workers home with sheets of waxed paper. In the evening hours, they would iron the sheets into bags, which were filled with chips the next day, ironed shut, and shipped. Her packaging innovation allowed potato chips to be stored in a more stable and secure environment, keeping them fresh until they were opened and reducing crumbling. Now potato chips could be mass-marketed, making them a new convenience food. Scudder's company was also credited as the first to imprint "freshness" dates on their products, setting the standard, which is now mandatory for food products. By taking on the Operational Innovations necessary to solve her freshness problems, Scudder opened the door to Marketplace Innovations, such as the freshness dates, that strengthened her relationship with consumers and provided a decided competitive advantage.[3]

When cellophane and later glassine were invented, packaging was improved and more Marketplace Innovations came about.

In 1933, the first preprinted, waxed, glassine bag debuted, making branding possible. Bagged chips also meant self-service; no clerk was needed to measure and weigh, and consumers had choices—the brand wars were on. What's important to note at this point is that insight about what customers want (first-day freshness) and business insight (that moisture, air, and shipping cut down on shelf life and caused breakage) led to the packaging innovation that removed the barrier to business growth.

From Dusty Roads to Dynasty

It has now been about 158 years since George Crum's kitchen tantrum created what we now call potato chips. Since then, dozens of local companies have jumped on the bandwagon, and Operational Innovations based on inventions like the mechanical potato peeler and the continuous fryer spurred the fledgling industry on. But what would ultimately take it to a new level was an ambitious twenty-four-year-old route salesman for the Barrett Food Company, manufacturer of Gardner's Potato Chips, which was based in Atlanta, Georgia. The salesman was Herman W. Lay.

Lay was exceptional in many ways, but perhaps his greatest gift was his intuition and close connection with his customers. He began selling chips from the trunk of his car, going from one grocery store to the next, talking with owners and customers, and watching them eat his chips. He noted reactions, asked questions, listened to how the chips crunched, and observed the delight this caused. He watched customers pick through slightly burned chips and gravitate to the light, golden ones. He saw them lick their fingers and dive in for "just one more."

So good was he at knowing what he was selling and why, that he saw tremendous potential in the business. Later that year, he borrowed $100 to take over Barrett's small warehouse in Nashville, Tennessee, on a distributorship basis. Growth came rapidly. In 1933, he hired his first salesman, and the following year, he opened up six new sales routes. By 1936, he had hired twenty-five employees and added additional products by making his own peanut butter cracker and fried popcorn snacks. The pivotal year was 1938, when he raised $60,000 to buy a financially struggling Barrett, its plants in Atlanta, and the Gardner's brand name.[4] It was the beginning of a dynasty that would make Lay's potato chips synonymous with America's favorite snack food.

There are several key reasons why this young entrepreneur became the potato chip king when so many others remained mere princes. Most important were his intuition and faith in consumers and his desire to understand what they wanted. From the beginning, he spent time with his customers, paying more attention to what they were saying than to what they were buying, constantly building his knowledge and insight. He was equally adept at understanding the business case. It's said that he would put accounts receivable in one pocket and accounts payable in the other. He could tell just by patting his pockets how he was doing and whether or not he should buy more potatoes. In time, even though his operations obviously outgrew his pocket accounting, he didn't forget his basic principles.

Keeping to his belief that pleasing consumers was paramount to success, he innovated a sales system that prompted people in the field to do more than merely deliver merchandise to store owners. They also stocked the merchandise, set up point-of-purchase displays, and helped ensure product quality by pulling stale bags off the shelves and displays before they could be sold and disappoint the customer. This "storedoor" delivery system helped increase revenues because salespeople were able to work a territory more thoroughly, building relationships and loyalty. What's more, when new products were introduced, acceptance and precious shelf space were easier to come by. This new delivery system, which started out as an Operational Innovation, was so revolutionary that it cascaded upward to become a Transformational Innovation that changed the way companies operated across the entire global food industry. They called the sales model direct store delivery (DSD), and today, more than eighty years later, it still defines the way companies deliver perishable food.

Lay was on a roll. During the early 1940s, he added four manufacturing plants and built a new plant in Atlanta that featured a continuous potato chip production line, one of the first in the world. In 1949, he established a research laboratory to develop new products with only one goal in mind: to manufacture the crunchiest, freshest, most golden-colored, longest-shelf-life snack on the market.

To accomplish this, the company became vertically integrated, working with farmers to develop the best potatoes with the lowest sugar content (sugar produces brown spots) from seeds. Researchers determined the best size and shape, the right region for each season, and new storage techniques to help keep potatoes robust through the winter months. Precision cutting techniques for consistent size, and frying oils vetted for taste and shelf life were developed. Salting techniques and speedy packaging were also refined with the same goal in mind—keeping first-day freshness for as long as possible.

From the plain chip, innovation in flavor evolved, influenced once again by the consumer. Watching how people ate chips dipped in sauces and dips inspired sour cream and onion and barbecue-style chips. The popularity of Hidden Valley Ranch salad dressing started a whole new flavor craze, and Marketplace Innovation—a connect-the-dots insight that Lay was particularly good at.

Through it all, the company kept perfecting production techniques. The specific guidelines for making the perfect chip are staggering and precisely controlled. Much of this science and technology came out of Lay's passion for serving customers while building a business that would thrive. And it did thrive—to the tune of five thousand pounds of potato chips processed an hour! This is a perfect example of continued building in areas where the technology (what), customer (who), and business (why) innovation circles overlap and intersect to catapult business to a new level.

In 1956, Lay took the company public with a workforce exceeding a thousand, manufacturing facilities in eight cities, and branches or warehouses in thirteen cities. Revenues in 1957 stood at $16 million, making Lay's the largest maker of potato chips in the United States. Today, the worldwide market for chips is over $16 *billion*.[5] Current retail sales of potato chips in the United States alone tops $6 billion per year. Potato chips are one of the most universal foods on the planet and one of the few products that don't need changes to flavor or design to suit different cultural tastes. Today, Lay's remains the world's number one brand of potato chips.

And it all started with a customer complaint.

This story has focused on how keeping the customer (who) front and center, pairing the resulting insights with the right technology (what), and having a solid business foundation (why) can lead to phenomenal innovation. It's about being able to imagine innovation possibilities at all four levels and having the foresight, courage, and leadership to take it all to the highest possible level. On the surface, it seems almost simplistic. A customer complained; the potato chip was born; and inventions, innovations, and astute business practices birthed a new empire. In practice, however, it takes a highly complex mosaic of skills, circumstances, and leadership to navigate the ship to the right shores.

Innovation is about progress, and if we can learn anything from the potato chip, it's that continuing opportunities and points of leverage are available to any brand. You just have to build on the right insights, invest in the right opportunities, and manage your risk by ensuring that all three circles—who, what, and why—are well aligned. When you marry that model to the four levels of innovation, you have the opportunity to create something as memorable as the taste of salt on your lips or the sound of golden crispness in your ears.

Innovation should be everyone's destiny.

For those who say times have changed and opportunities are fewer than they were in Herman Lay's time, we say, "Not so!" If anything, there are more opportunities than ever. We are in a time of evolutionary change. Insight and reach within the marketplace *is* greater than ever for those who look. Technology is evolving faster than ever for those who want to embrace it, and the reins of leadership are waiting for those who have the courage to take them up. There's a bridge that spans the gap between what can be imagined and what can be realized, and that bridge is leadership, which is where we're going next.

PART 2

THE LEADERSHIP EQUATION

f you ask people what the biggest obstacle to innovation is, they won't say technology or ideas or even opportunity; they'll tell you it's people. Senior managers say their people don't care. They're not showing initiative or enterprise. Their people say they're micromanaged and processed to death, that they're not empowered to try out new ideas, and if they do try and fail, it's their heads. Everyone blames everyone else for their company's lack of innovation, or what one midlevel manager calls "nonovation."

The truth is that everyone is right—at least in part. Employees do think it's risky, or at the very least not a priority, to be looking for new ideas to keep the company growing. An online survey conducted in 2006-2007 showed that fully 33 percent of workers believe their bosses are not even open to innovation ideas.[1] This belief and the lethargy it creates make senior managers right; their people aren't trying. So what's the answer?

The person at the top.

Sine qua non. That's Latin for "without which there is none," which is to say that without leadership, there is no innovation. The person at the top is the one who provides vision, sets expectations, and empowers the imagination of the entire company. If leadership doesn't own innovation, innovation won't happen. It's as simple as that.

You'll be seeing this idea repeated often in the following chapters, as we delve into what defines success in innovation leadership. First, we'll look at how different leadership agendas can have an explosive impact on a company for better or worse. To do this, we chose four companies—Ford, Toyota, Apple, and Hasbro—and examined different leadership eras in each company. The proof is in the pudding, as they say, so we decided we might as well examine real companies with actual track records rather than conduct a hypothetical experiment.

Later, we'll look at what makes a successful leader tick. Is it, as a *New York Times* article reports, "attention to detail, persistence, efficiency, analytic thoroughness, and the ability to work long hours"?[2] Is it true that these "organized, dogged, anal-retentive, and slightly boring people are more likely to thrive"?[3] The answer is no—and yes.

Most successful people share characteristics like persistence and dedication, but innovation leadership does take a different type of personality and way of thinking that we'll explore. In the process, we'll see how both the dramatic Steve Jobs and the humble A. G. Lafley can be masters of innovation leadership.

Finally, we'll look at leadership from a more global perspective. The CEO might need to own innovation, but he or she can't do it alone. To succeed, you not only have to have the right stuff, the people around you have to have it too. In the last chapter of Part 2, we'll look at the characteristics of leadership as they relate to the four types of innovation. We'll also take a first look at culture and how it can either help leaders thrive or leave them wilting on the vine. By the end of this section, we guarantee you'll see yourself and those around you in a very different light.

CHAPTER 5

The Role of Leadership in Innovation

The Buck Starts Here

Innovation fuels the engine of growth.
Leadership delivers the fuel.

—JANE STEVENSON

While innovation is conceived in inspiration, it can become a reality only through leadership. It's the glue that cements the connected dots and turns a great idea into a commercial success. A company's level of innovation is therefore a direct reflection of its top leadership. If word from above is cautious and focused on containing costs and beefing up the bottom line, then employees and partners see things in terms of managing what they already have and judging it by today's standards. If leadership is focused on innovation, however, it's a very different picture—one of a company with a future anchored in profitable growth and endless possibilities.

Chief executive officer and generic drug visionary Eli Hurvitz is a case in point. Early in his career, Hurvitz envisioned a strategic plan to enter the generic drug market in a global way. At that time, because of strict regulation, only 35 percent of off-patent drugs had generic competitors. But proposed legislation to soften regulation in the United States was expected to change that dramatically. Hurvitz envisioned huge potential. In fact, he was so sure of his strategy that moving his company, Teva Pharmaceuticals, into this space became his primary focus. Despite the fact that the company didn't have much in the way of expansion capital or even the expertise to take on such a venture, the relatively new CEO pressed on. Looking to the American market, where uniform regulations offered a more simplified entry into generics than Europe, where rules varied from country to country, he went shopping for the best deal he could find. Whether it was luck or incredible insight, his timing was perfect.

In 1984, the legislation passed and Hurvitz found his deal. It turned out to be a joint venture with WR Grace to acquire a German-owned, U.S.-based company called Lemon. On paper, there wasn't much to admire about the company, but the price was right and it fit perfectly into Hurvitz's carefully developed strategy to break into the U.S. market. Grace invested $21.5 million, while Hurvitz only had to put up $1.5 million. This was a good thing, considering what was ahead. "We had to change everything," Hurvitz said. "Management, accounting, language, product—people laughed at us. But I had a vision and we had a strategy!" In the end, refusing to give up paid off. In 2000, the company reported $1 billion in sales. Today, it's $3 billion every quarter.[1]

Hurvitz went on to lead the company for another twenty-five years as CEO, and in 2002, he became chairman of the board. Under his determined and sometimes controversial stewardship,

Teva became a pioneer for a new flagship industry. While the category has exploded with new players, Teva is still ranked as one of the world's largest generic drug manufacturers.

By recognizing an opportunity for a major category breakthrough and then doggedly leading it to market, Hurvitz built a critical bridge between an idea for innovation and the leadership needed to see it through. His passion and commitment to what he believed was possible was the driver that enabled his leadership team to do things they might not otherwise have imagined. It's not enough to have a vision—you have to inspire others to dream with you. That's what makes a great innovation leader and what separates innovation companies from those that just survive from day to day, hoping for a brighter future.

Throughout Part 1, we gave you examples of companies that have changed the world, birthed industries, and brought profitability to their shareholders. While each company had its own way of getting there, the one common thread that made success possible was leadership. The buck doesn't just stop at the top; it starts there too. Without innovation-focused leadership, sustainable growth just isn't possible.

In this opening chapter about leadership, we'll see what a difference the CEO makes in the real world by looking at four different companies and the various leaders who influenced their fates. Some of these individuals have fostered great innovations, while others have left their companies either standing still or, worse yet, facing ruin. Next, we'll do something a bit different. In talking with people about this book, we asked them what they would tell a CEO if they could. Their replies moved us in unexpected ways. They were candid, emotional, and rich with insight, as you will see in the letter that closes this chapter.

What we do as leaders has a great impact on people—employees, customers, shareholders, and stakeholders. Too often, we lose site of the ripple effect of our actions and attitudes. Yet those ripples, whether great or small, can determine the fate of so many.

If you want to see your company win, to see it break away from the rest of the pack with sustainable growth through innovation, you have to be the driver.

The Leadership Imperative

In 1978, James McGregor Burns wrote, "One of the most universal cravings of our time is a hunger for compelling and creative leadership."[2] Traditionally, leaders have been defined as those who hold power, which allows presidents, prime ministers, and military generals—regardless of their accomplishments—to be considered leaders. Equating leadership with management has further confused the issue. Someone like John D. Rockefeller, who was an adept manager, is considered an accomplished leader because of the economic power he amassed. But if a leader focuses only on building power or managing for wealth, he or she will never be able to forge a new path for others to follow.

Innovation leadership is about inspiring a mind-set that opens your organization up to discovery. It's about developing the framework that supports an innovation strategy and empowering people to make the right choices on their paths. Perhaps most of all, innovation leadership is about convincing people they can do things they don't think they can. When people know their role in innovation and are engaged in the growth of a company, there's nothing they can't accomplish. On the other hand, when confusion, personal competition, politics, or ruthlessness rules, it's everyone for themselves, and innovation is the last thing on anyone's mind.

The Two Faces of Ford

In 1999, when Jacques Nasser took the helm from Alex Trotman, Ford Motor Company was firing on all cylinders. Flush with cash and new products, it had 370,000 employees in two hundred countries, sales and revenues of $143 billion, record earnings of $6.6 billion, and a stock price of $65 per share.[3]

As the new CEO, Nasser had big dreams for Ford's expansion. Not only did he want the company, whose primary profit maker was trucks, to become a leader in the world car market, he also envisioned it as a provider of rental vehicles, auto repair, and satellite radio. In other words, he envisioned an empire. To this end, he oversaw the acquisition of Hertz and purchased Jaguar, Aston Martin, Volvo, and Land Rover as the crown jewels of his new Premier Auto Group (PAG).

This expansion project was his baby. He established glamorous regional offices in London's Berkeley Square and an imposing headquarters building in Irvine, California, that was powered by a high-tech fuel cell and had separate lobbies for each of the six companies. Customers for the individual brands were not to know about the existence of PAG, but the sub-branding was impressively massive. Journalists were wined and dined, expensive trips were organized, and there was even a quarterly PAG magazine printed on heavy art paper. Filled with photographs of beautiful people and their cars, it was an upgrade in image for the company that had been founded to serve the common man.

Nasser projected that PAG would be selling a million vehicles within ten years and delivering up to 80 percent of Ford's profit. The sky was the limit, and brands were everything. Volvo, he believed, would dominate America with sales of more than 650,000, and Jaguar would build the X-type and sell up to 800,000 cars a year globally.[4] Ultimately though, what Nasser envisioned was giving the world more glamorous versions of what it already had.

At the same time that PAG was being polished and shined, Nasser was also looking at the core business. In the first year, he closed money-losing plants, discontinued models that didn't generate desired profits, sold losing operations, and weeded out executives. He also put in place a human resources policy mandating that 10 percent of all workers receive a "C" grade, which could lead to termination. Nasser's justification for this was that new people, new philosophies, and new technologies were required to ensure Ford's success in the new economy.[5] Although CEOs, most notably Jack Welch, had used this approach in other companies, the changes weren't easy for Ford employees to accept. So in 2000, when Ford's flagship four-wheel-drive sport utility vehicle, the Explorer, was involved in numerous rollover accidents, the moral support Nasser needed to survive the crisis was gone, and it seemed his vision would never be realized. As the disaster unfolded, employee morale was shaken and Ford's famous quality image tarnished.

Two hundred deaths were ultimately linked to the Firestone Wilderness AT tires that were standard issue on the SUV. In the end, Ford committed itself to replacing millions of Firestone tires (in addition to the 6.5 million that Firestone replaced) at an after-tax cost of more than $2 billion.[6] But it was too little too late. Ford reported its first consecutive quarterly losses in nearly a decade, and stock prices plummeted.

The unfortunate Explorer incident soured Ford's fortunes and contributed to Nasser's removal in October 2001. When Bill Ford replaced Nasser as CEO, he announced that his first task would be to repair stakeholder relationships and go back to the basics of the car and truck business. He also made it clear that his intention for the automaker was innovation and growth.

This is an important point—intention is a powerful force in both leadership and innovation. When the intention at the top is to build a sustainable company that benefits everyone, decisions are made to further that intention. When it's about power, beating the competition, or even maintaining the status quo instead of improving for the customer, company, and stakeholders, decision making is completely different.

Following his tenure as CEO, during which Ford worked to build an innovation culture, finding someone who could carry on his vision of sustainable growth was top of mind for Bill Ford. If he had learned one thing running the company, it was that innovation too often got lost in day-to-day concerns and seldom survived internal politics. So when he went looking for a new leader, he wasn't just looking for a talented executive, he was searching for a partner in spirit, someone who could reinvent and reimagine an entire corporate culture focused on innovation. He found his man in the number-two chair at the aircraft manufacturer Boeing.

The choice of Alan Mulally shocked industry observers. Never had someone with absolutely no car experience been appointed to such a high position. But the creator of the Boeing 777 had what Ford needed, and he wasted little time proving his worth. Sensing long before his crosstown rivals that the automotive business was about to get extremely difficult, Mulally's first task was to ensure that Ford had enough cash on hand to weather a recessionary storm. He did this by mortgaging all of the company's assets, including the blue oval logo itself, on Wall Street and netted $23.5 billion. "I spoke to a room with over five hundred bankers," he recalls. "Why did they give us the money? Because we had a plan."[7]

That plan included fixing an insular, backstabbing executive culture that included fiefdoms spread around the globe that paralyzed the company's decision making. Mulally managed to unite these competing factions (or send them packing) and establish an executive team whose members actually work together for a common purpose. Ford is also fully leveraging its worldwide capabilities, finally bringing the popular Fiesta and the new global Focus sold in Europe to America.

All of what Mulally has done to move the company forward would be impressive at any time, but it's nearly miraculous today. Unlike its two Detroit rivals, Ford didn't declare bankruptcy and hasn't dipped its hand into the Troubled Asset Relief Program trough for bailout money. It stands as the only one of the Big Three American automakers that is still an independent entity. And while it's not out of the woods, by mid-2010, it had posted a $4.7 billion profit and begun reducing debt.[8]

Ford and Mulally are living proof that extraordinary leaders with vision and determination really can make all the difference to an organization. This is especially true when a leader has the support of his board. Ford Motor Company is in a position to succeed not only because of the company Mulally has rebuilt but because of the one Bill Ford has envisioned. The chairman is passionate about innovation and making Ford's vehicles more fuel-efficient. By investing in a number of technologies, including electrification, biofuels, fuel cells, and more efficient gas engines, the company is securing future growth. By increasing spending on innovation when everyone else was cutting back, it ensured sustainability. That's where its future lies. Despite the company's precarious financial position, it has a good chance of making it, because unlike a decade ago, its focus isn't on power—it's on innovation.

The Toyota Way

It's impossible to talk about Ford without turning an eye to one of its chief rivals—Toyota. While the Ford Motor Company was going through its crisis in both the market and internal ranks, the Japanese automaker was making fistfuls of dollars rolling across the globe with its well-positioned cars for the middle class and its innovative hybrid Prius. It seemed the company could do no wrong. Toyota was clearly the darling of the press, with a management model even Bill Gates admired. A 2007 *New York Times* article titled "From 0 to 60 to World Domination" pretty much said it all. But while the company was wrapping up the globe—in 2003, it hit the 6 million mark in production—it was also setting itself up for a massive disaster.

One of the hallmarks of Toyota was incredible quality. This is what the company was built on and where many of its innovations took place. From concept to dealership to driveway, it continually improved and innovated its way to market domination. But with growth comes new challenges, and this is where Toyota stumbled. To boost profitability, Katsuaki Watanabe—the company's president from 2005 to 2009—pressured his engineers to cut costs aggressively. They did, and the cost-saving measures seemed to be successful. But as so often happens when top leaders are primarily interested in saving money, other considerations like quality and innovation fell by the wayside.[9]

This was particularly sad for a company that had always been respected for both its quality and its management principles, a company that in some ways honored the best of innovation. Dubbed "The Toyota Way,"[10] its doctrine embodies a set of principles and behaviors that underlie the company's managerial approach and production system. At the core of the Toyota Way are two principles: continuous improvement and respect for people. The first encourages establishing a long-term vision, working on challenges, innovating continually, and going to the source of an issue or a problem. The second, respect for people, relates to making every effort to understand each other, take responsibility, and do everything possible to build mutual trust. It also fosters teamwork, personal and professional growth, and sharing opportunities to maximize individual and team performance. Both of these principles are core to innovation leadership, but saying them and living them are two different things—and many companies fail to do both.

When quality issues directly related to cost-cutting measures started cropping up, Toyota set aside its own rulebook. As customers began to raise questions about the quality of its vehicles, either because they performed unsafely or just didn't look good, Toyota was slow to respond. "It was as if we were engaged in car manufacturing in a virtual world and became insensitive to vehicle failings and defects in the market," Akio Toyoda, Toyota's current CEO, said later.[11] This reportedly happened both because the reporting system from foreign buyers didn't get to Toyota City leaders, and because the very thought of a quality failure within the company seemed impossible. After all, Toyota was the quality leader. Letting customers down wasn't the Toyota Way.

The writing on the wall was clear, however. In 2009, after only four years at the helm, Watanabe was replaced by Akio Toyoda—grandson of the company's founder. When Toyoda took on the job, he immediately announced that he was taking the company "back to basics." Unfortunately, those basics don't seem to include innovation. While Ford shows clear commitment to transforming transportation, Toyota has passed on the latest battery technology to save money, and it doesn't seem particularly concerned about leading the way on all-electric cars, even though other manufacturers are intent on developing this market.

Toyota insists no organizational or cultural changes are necessary—it just took its eye off the ball and is now refocused on earning back its former status. In this regard, Ford handled itself better than Toyota. Within a short time of taking over, Bill Ford took steps to heal internal and external damage and set a course for innovation based on a much more solid foundation. Only time will tell, but Toyota could still find itself where General Motors was thirty years ago: with a seemingly dominant market position but a culture that so weakens the company that it eventually collapses. Much will depend on whether or not going back to basics eventually includes a desire to once again lead through innovation and whether the company ultimately lives a leadership model that frees its employees' considerable talent to bring the company to new heights.

Apple: Killer Innovation, Killer Profits

If there's one company that knows how important having the right leader for innovation is, it's certainly Apple. Now considered to be one of the most innovative companies of our time, it wasn't always so. In 1985, when Steve Jobs was ousted from the company after butting heads with CEO John Sculley, Apple lost its innovation soul. Though 1989 through 1991 were profitable years, the company started faltering with product failures, most notably the resource-intensive Newton, the forerunner to the personal digital assistant, that Sculley had banked on. When money tightened in the early nineties, a sweeping round of empire building occurred, where midlevel managers tried to take over as many projects as possible to keep those projects alive. The result was a rash of new offerings in so many different markets, from education to home use, that consumers were totally confused.[12]

Sculley was a wiz at marketing know-how, but the product confusion and lack of technology vision were starting to take its toll. These failures, coupled with declining stock prices, ended his reign. Sculley was replaced by Michael Spindler (1993–1996), who in turn was followed by Gil Amelio (1996–1997). Neither CEO had much luck in turning the company around, but Amelio is credited with raising the white flag. Struggling to come up with the new technology the company needed to stay alive, Amelio approached Jobs to purchase NeXT, the company Jobs had founded after leaving Apple. Steve was back.

While some see Jobs as arrogant and autocratic, it can't be denied that he is able to see future technology through a marketing prism. Often criticized for his leadership style, his achievements are still the stuff of legend. Since his return to Apple, he has built a culture based on brand fanaticism, radical customer devotion, and killer products that make killer profits. Employees often say they're afraid of him, but despite feeling intimidated, they share his vision of reality for the company. Without a doubt, one of his greatest talents is his ability to express ideas to teams for realization and then to inspire them to achieve what seems unachievable.

Within a year of Jobs' return, Apple was on its legendary comeback track. In 1998, Jobs introduced the iMac. Built from the ground up with the masses in mind, its simplicity set the tone for generations of new products from the iPod to the iPad. Within ninety days of its launch, the iMac accounted for 7.1 percent of total PC unit sales, beating out the top-selling Compaq Presario and achieving with one product what Sculley had tried to do with a dozen.[13]

This put the company back on the business map, and Apple hasn't looked back since. Neither has Jobs. For him, innovation isn't just a passion, it's a mandate, and that's what sets him apart from so many leaders. It's not enough to be *at* the top; you have to *own* the top. Without a determined innovation leader directing the show, you not only handicap your future, you also leave yourself wide open to competitive assault.

From Oh, No! to Go, Hasbro!

Hasbro, the number-two toy company in the world, has been through an evolution of leadership that has seen the organization move from an environment happy with maintaining the status quo to one on the cutting edge of continuing innovation. Founded in 1923 as a textile remnant company, Hasbro faced one of its greatest challenges in 1996, when Mattel launched a takeover bid. Though it failed, the attempted coup sent a signal—things needed to change.

Looking to revitalize itself, Hasbro brought in an outside consultant who rearranged parts of the organization, but without the direction of a strong innovation strategy, its traditional brands were neglected. Instead, the toy maker chased hot licenses tied to movies such as *Star Wars* and *Batman*. It also suffered from internal competition, with divisions acting like unruly siblings and fighting each other for attention.

The reckoning came in 2000, when company revenue fell more than 10 percent to $3.8 billion, and it lost $144.6 million. Fighting to regain its footing, Hasbro turned to an old ally, Alfred Verrecchia, who had been with the company for thirty-eight years in a variety of finance and operating roles. Verrecchia was promoted to president in 2000, and he quickly initiated crucial changes. These included moving all the far-flung toy divisions to headquarters in Pawtucket, Rhode Island, to cut costs and get them to work together; reducing $1.2 billion in long-term debt; and focusing on the extension of Hasbro's main brands, such as G.I. Joe, Monopoly, and the Easy-Bake Oven. In 2003, he was appointed CEO. His leadership helped complete a turnaround that centered primarily on reinvigorating Hasbro's classic toys and games and adapting its lineup to the increasing influence of electronics. Between 2003 and Verrecchia's retirement in 2008, stock prices increased 60 percent, net income more than doubled, and sales climbed 22 percent.[14]

Central to Verrecchia's success was a young visionary who joined the company in 2000. We first introduced Brian Goldner in Chapter 2, where we talked about his success in taking Transformers from a $30 million product to a $500 million core brand. It was no surprise then that the CEO mantel passed to him on Verrecchia's retirement. Goldner had earned the job, and he was perfect for it. In the years that followed, Goldner implemented a strategy that is still leading to sustainable growth, even during the economic downturn. In 2010, the company gave him a raise and a new contract to keep him on board.

A Letter to Leaders

For nearly a century, Hasbro has made it through the ups and downs of leadership, and through leadership it still has a bright future. It wasn't always on track, but it managed to find its way as most of the companies we've talked about have. What Ford, Apple, and Hasbro have in common is someone at the top who believes in innovation, has the courage to champion it, and has the desire for everyone involved to win—not for power, domination, control, or ego—but for customer and company.

We started off by saying that leadership is the glue that cements the innovation dots for a true innovation company to follow. Without that leadership—well, we've seen what can happen, and we suspect you have too.

You wouldn't be reading this book if you didn't want innovation to be part of your company and if you didn't want to facilitate change. So now we'd like you to find a quiet place to finish reading this chapter. Turn off your phone, get comfortable, and tune out the distractions that constantly compete for your attention. We want to share something very special with you: the thoughts and feelings of people who work for someone just like you—your employees. Candid, emotional, and hopeful, these may be the most important words you read for a long time to come.

Dear CEO:

You hold the keys to our destiny. As your employees, our future depends on you, so we wanted to share our thoughts. As the company's chief architect, you set the tone for everything. If you design a business based on cost cutting or productivity, we'll stay focused on what already exists, trying to do things cheaper, faster, and better, but without an eye on the future. If you envision a business based on growth and innovation, we'll be unleashed to build and create. That's what we want—to unite in creating an exciting future beyond what any of us could imagine individually.

We're committed to doing well, both for ourselves and the company. But we need your leadership to achieve something great and sustainable. We want to play full out, using all the talents we have to contribute to the world. In the end though, we can measure our success only by the yardstick you provide.

If the measure is doing what we're told, then we'll be careful to do just that. If you set a vision that excites us and measures us by our ability to take things as far as we can, we'll stretch.

In addition to vision and encouragement, we need resources. As the leader, you control all the resources available in our organization. They can either be used to create groundbreaking innovation and market supremacy, or they can be micromanaged, diminished, and underutilized. Which scenario ultimately plays out depends on the culture you create. It will either focus us on business possibilities with an abundance mentality, or it will keep us contained by fear. If it's the latter, we *will* use our political skills to compete for limited resources, putting an endless internally competitive game into play. While we're good at it, that's not what we want.

We want to be part of something that encourages us to move beyond imagined limitations. We want to be proud of you and feel honored to be a part of this company. We want to believe in what this company can accomplish, not just for ourselves, but for the world. Please call us to a level of greatness.

Growing the company requires that all of us, especially you, become courageous explorers. Without exploration, there's no discovery, and without discovery, there's no innovation. That means not being afraid to fail. We're willing to challenge ourselves enough to ensure that we do sometimes fail. And when we do, we want to feel proud that we took a chance and that we learned and grew from our mistakes. Your understanding and appreciation when we take risks will ensure that we continue to give it our all and that we don't slink away in fear of reprisal for having tried.

When people see you or someone on your team annihilate an associate for taking a risk, it ensures that very few of us will try to expand our boundaries. We're sure you've seen this type of degradation or felt its sting yourself. The ongoing fear this creates keeps everyone from thinking independently. When that happens, you have to direct or micromanage us to get anything done. Even with your energy, you can't hope to direct and evaluate the work of thousands of people.

Instead of intimidation, what we want and need is a safe environment where we can risk the occasional failure and speak openly to help the company achieve its goals. In this environment, we'll have the passion and commitment needed to make our company extraordinary instead of just average or even mediocre.

You have the power to make it happen if you remember to *own* your own power. So much is under your control, and using that power wisely is one of your greatest responsibilities. Watch the people inside the company and see if they're acting empowered or just telling you what you want to hear. If the latter is true, you'll need to better harness your power to achieve your goals. Diversity of thinking is vital to creating an environment of innovation and growth, and you don't want to lose that advantage!

We so want to be excited about the vision you create, and we hope you'll share it in a way we can relate to. We want to know our role in making it happen. If we don't get the message because it's wrapped up in pressure to perform to number-mired standards instead of achievements, then we'll all fail. We understand there's tremendous pressure to cut costs and promote efficiency. We agree that operational efficiency can't be ignored, but there are people in our organization who can manage the processes necessary to "do things right." What these people can't do is provide the leadership that determines "what the right things to do are." That's your sole responsibility.

Demonstrate that innovation is a priority by providing the needed funds and visibility for people to see that what you say is true. Actions speak louder than words. If you take risks to move the company forward through innovation and growth, we will too. We're all in this together—or at least we should be.

In the past, many of us have been troubled by the amount of time we spend on keeping innovation from moving backward instead of moving it forward. We've worked for people who had great potential to be innovation leaders, yet they weren't able to capitalize on their promise commercially. We don't want this to happen to you. Creating a culture that has successful innovation at its core will deliver big dividends. We believe that, with you, we can build a world-class organization that is united and focused on winning in the marketplace, not just internally.

One last thing: the most respected leaders we know have come to their role with the humility of a servant. As a CEO who serves, you will empower your people to do amazing things. Believe in what you're doing; believe in what can be done; and stay open, excited, and driven to achieve an inspired vision. You're not in this alone, but *you are the only one who can make it happen*, because the buck doesn't just start with you—it ends there too.

Sincerely,

Your People

CHAPTER 6

Portrait of an Innovation Leader

Mirror, Mirror on the Wall

Good leaders have the confidence to dream
big dreams and the ability to get others
to make those dreams a reality.

—DALE MORRISON, CEO, MCCAIN FOODS

What do the parachute, the helicopter, the airplane, *The Last Supper*, the first war tank, the swinging bridge, and the *Mona Lisa* have in common? Here's a clue. All of them came about in the fifteenth century during what was arguably the beginning of the modern era—and all of them were conceived by just one person. Known as the ultimate Renaissance man, he was also the ultimate innovator.

A rare blend of artist, scientist, and inventor, Leonardo da Vinci envisioned—and his talented hand sketched, painted, and annotated—thousands of ideas and observations that centuries later became reality. Fascinated with just about everything, legend has it that he studied flight by attaching a pair of homemade wings to a lizard and pitching it off a roof.

Clearly he was a genius, but what intrigues us about him isn't so much *what* he did as *how* he did it. Combining both science and art in his thinking, he brought the full power of his mind to bear on whatever challenge he sought to unravel. This type of analytical/creative or whole-brain thinking was a significant part of da Vinci's brilliance. Combine this with characteristics like vision, courage, and tenacity, and you begin to see a portrait emerge of what it takes to be an extraordinary innovation leader today.

In this chapter, we'll look at what separates legendary leaders from capable captains of commerce by looking at four critical elements: (1) capabilities and characteristics; (2) affiliations and team building; (3) whole-brain thinking; and (4) sustainability. As we build this portrait, think about those companies and leaders you admire as being the best and how they compare with the snapshots presented here. See if you can find the stamp of leadership in the innovations they've fostered. Strong leaders will always shape the company in their image. When a leader's vision is to foster innovation, both the leader as the artist and the company as the canvas can come together to create an extraordinary masterpiece. But before you can create that masterpiece, you first have to imagine it.

The Artist's Pallet—Capabilities and Characteristics

Every artist needs the tools to execute what the mind can envision. For innovation leaders, these tools take the form of certain characteristics and capabilities that enable leaders to do their jobs more naturally and effectively. To understand your potential, you need to know who you are as a leader and how that impacts your innovation effectiveness. Once you recognize where you're strongest and where you need support, you can make sure your team effectively complements your strengths and constraints.

TABLE 6.1 **Key Leadership Characteristics**

KEY LEADERSHIP CHARACTERISTICS	ROLE IN INNOVATION
Confident	You're comfortable in your own skin and not afraid to be vulnerable. You don't need to have all the answers personally to move ahead.
Intuitive, creative, and visionary	You have the ability to envision tomorrow before it gets here. You can sense the path for moving forward based on strong intuitive instincts.
Provocative	You're curious and ask illuminating questions. You're always looking to align the team based on the fullest knowledge of the most current facts.
Good at listening	You have the ability to absorb information like a sponge. You hear behind the words to what people are really saying.
Genuine and trusted	You insist on clarity and avoid hidden agendas. You keep the environment uncluttered by fear and politics. Everyone knows you're focused on real work and that you're who you say you are and will do what you say you will.

continued

TABLE 6.1 **Key Leadership Characteristics** *continued*

KEY LEADERSHIP CHARACTERISTICS	ROLE IN INNOVATION
Courageous	You're willing to make big bets for the future. You won't protect the past at the expense of moving forward. You have persistence and determination; "failure until success" is your motto.
Nurturing to others	You create an environment that focuses on the positive and supports people's development.
Determined to win and win together	While highly competitive, you're not territorial. You embrace diversity of thinking and encourage input from everyone.
Spiritual with strong values	You're passionate and your belief in what you are doing must be strong enough and compelling enough to be accepted by others. Your vision should be contagious for long-term success.
Tenacious	You stay on course, even when things are not going well. You don't give up; you adapt and stay focused on the ultimate goal.
Possessing a high level of urgency	You understand the importance of speed in innovation. You're not afraid to act, and you keep others on track to do so as well. You know you must multitask inside your own mind.
Pragmatic and disciplined in approach	You know when to hold them and when to fold them. You connect the dots and bring things together.
Humble	You put pride aside and are willing to admit when you're wrong.

The list in Table 6.1 isn't complete, of course, but the more essential characteristics you possess, the higher your chances for success will be. You'll notice one thing that isn't on the list is a high profile. There are leaders who achieve rock-star status, like Jack Welsh, Bill Gates, and Steve Jobs. However, we've found many others who embody the essential characteristics and have set their companies on a true innovation path without much fanfare. For instance, take Murray Martin of Pitney Bowes.

In Martin's role as chief executive officer and president, he has full strategic and operational responsibility for the company and its sustainable growth through innovation. Under his leadership, Pitney Bowes has produced major technological innovations of a transformational nature in the mailing industry, including a number of active patents with applications in printing, shipping, encryption, and financial services.

Since Martin's appointment as chief operating officer in September 2004 and through his tenure as the company's president and CEO, Pitney Bowes has maintained an ongoing program of productivity initiatives to enhance its ability to go to market, reduce its cost structure, and improve profitability. It has increased revenue through an acquisition strategy that has given it a presence in markets adjacent to the mail stream, including software, mail services, and marketing services, as well as an expanding international presence.

This has been no easy feat for a company that had to reinvent itself several times to stay ahead of the ever-changing technology curve. Over the past ninety years, Pitney Bowes developed the first postage meter to be approved by the U.S. Postal Service (creating, in essence, a new form of currency); the first mailing equipment to enable two-dimensional bar coding for postal payments; and the first in-line weighing and metering system. All of these inventions centered around mail and, in particular, envelopes.

"For most of our history, we've focused on products that related in some way to the envelope. It's a valuable piece of real estate," notes Martin. "Addresses, postage, return address, sealing, folding of mail to insert—if it goes in it or on it, we're interested. That's what's driven us. We looked at it and thought, how many pennies are there in the handling of that envelope? What do we need to do to get every penny out?

"Today, however, we know we have to look beyond products. Things will change significantly for us over the next ten years as society and technology evolves. I already know our innovation will migrate from products to solutions to information. The next Transformational Innovation we're looking toward is monitoring the delivery, versus the currency, of each piece of physical mail. That's a developing direction, but what I try to cultivate in my people and myself is the ability to see the future and envision its form. Along with a no-boundary outlook—past, present, or future—that's what allows for the thinking that creates tomorrow to occur. If you focus only on continuous improvement without an eye toward innovation, it won't be long before you realize that current success isn't enough to ensure the future."

Painting the Picture

Martin brings up one of the most important capabilities of innovation leadership: the ability to inspire and convey your vision in a compelling way. In other words, great leaders also need to be great communicators. They inspire not just internally, but outside the company as well. This gift is critical to success, and if you can get your employees to see what you see for the future and believe in their ability to get there, you're well on your way to realizing your vision.

When Bilal arrived at Frito Lay, Roger Enrico had already moved on. But when Enrico was heading up the business, the Eagle brand of potato chips was eating Frito Lay alive! Lay's was rapidly losing market share, and Enrico knew that had to change. So he laid out the vision, strategy, and execution plan with a capable team. Then, most important, he communicated his vision in a way that zeroed in on the key priorities and activated the organization at large.

To do this, Enrico drew on one of his considerable talents— his capacity to share his vision in a tactical, day-to-day way. People who were there say he always shared his strategy in short, highly memorable phrases. He spoke to each individual in a way that related to his or her daily responsibilities, all without being highly prescriptive. For example, in the battle to win back Lay's market share from Eagle, he introduced the mantra, "Let's take back the streets." For sales, those words meant, "Let's make sure our stores are merchandized properly and priced competitively." For the marketers, they meant, "I need to create the brand power that drives every consumer to Lay's products." For the innovation leaders, taking back the streets meant they had to ensure that the taste and packaging of Lay's products were so compelling that consumers couldn't live without them. Once Enrico activated the hearts and minds of everybody in the organization, the market share was as good as theirs. Today, Eagle chips are no longer available. The company went out of business.

It was a simple thing: "Take back the streets." Yet it empowered an entire company and became part of its DNA. Everyone knew that winning was not up to just one person; it was everybody's job. They understood on a deep level that the only way to achieve maximum success was to work together. If you, as a leader, can achieve this kind of alignment in your workforce, your organization will achieve what before seemed impossible.

The Power of Team

Enrico could have been the most powerful communicator in the world, but if he hadn't had a powerful team to work with, he might have taken back a block or two, but he wouldn't have reclaimed the kingdom. Whether you're the CEO, like Enrico, or you lead in a matrix-oriented role, the power of your team is the true power of your leadership—especially if you are looking to innovate and grow. This point was vivid in our conversation with Angela Ahrendts, chief executive officer of Burberry.

As Ahrendts tells it, she and Christopher Bailey, chief creative director, worked together at Donna Karan International and accomplished amazing things there. A few years later, Bailey moved to Burberry with the experience of having already helped an outstanding CEO get a company moving forward with some momentum. When Burberry looked to recruit a CEO successor, Bailey suggested Ahrendts. While the process was driven by the board and then-CEO Rose Marie Bravo, Ahrendts felt as if she was actually recruited by Bailey. They talked about what they would do if they were "running the show." It was conversational dreaming at the time, or so they thought. Recalling their time at Donna Karan, they reminded one another that they could create the company of the future as they had dreamed of many years before. This idea captivated Ahrendts's imagination. Here was a chance to work with Bailey and others to create an innovation-driven environment that would use the skills and capabilities of every associate in the company. So compelling was the idea that she picked up her family and moved them to London.

This close association of leaders and team members was clear in every successful innovation project we reviewed for this book. Dale Morrison of McCain Foods has a CEO innovation council (CIC) made up of his direct reports, who head up the company's regional businesses around the world; the head of innovation; and the chief supply chain officer. This group guides McCain's focus on "fewer, bigger, and better" ideas.

When Morrison took over as CEO, he was handed a company that had been successful for fifty years by just keeping up with demand. Then things changed, as they did for many of us.

Instead of simply meeting demand, the organization now had to create it proactively. For that, it needed innovation and a leader who knew what was necessary to make it happen.

"I think a lot of what defines successful innovation is also what defines a good leader—period," says Morrison. "Leadership is the 'secret sauce,' so to speak. Good CEOs have the confidence to dream big dreams and the ability to get others to engage and support them in making those dreams a reality. To do that, you have to know your customers and the external environment you operate in and be able to paint a picture of a different future. It's also about making sure you have the right team that can execute, manage costs, get innovations to market quickly, and achieve business results.

"Right now, we're investing an enormous amount of time, effort, and energy in building an organization of leaders. That's how we'll keep this going and growing beyond any one person." We couldn't have said it better ourselves. What Morrison so succinctly points out are the key capabilities and characteristics that every leader should have, regardless of the type or size of his or her business. Morrison's skill in maximizing his own capabilities and inspiring others to do the same has resulted in 13 percent of the company's growth coming from innovation.

As a leader, you need to develop an organizational structure that accommodates your team and works within the innovation culture and structure of your business. To assess the team health of your organization, answer the following set of questions. Be as honest as possible in your assessment and get outside validation to make sure what you believe to be true is actually the case. Are you ready? What kind of team support do you have?

1. Does everyone in your organization personally understand its vision and strategy?
2. Does each member of your team view you as the ultimate decision maker or tiebreaker in setting innovation priorities and assigning key resources?

3. Can team members connect their actions with cause and effect?
4. Can they directly connect their contribution to the company's top-line growth?
5. Do you celebrate successes and learn from failures?
6. Is your team diverse in its thinking?
7. How flexible and nimble is your organization?
8. Is your team able to discuss and debate issues openly and without fear?
9. Do team members support each other's initiatives?

When you have the answers to these questions you'll have a better idea of how ready you and your team are, not only to create an innovation culture, but also to be able to activate innovation down the road.

Broadening Your Circle—Affiliation

The pace in today's world is nonstop, full of imperatives and limited energy. Just keeping your teams energized and getting to the people you *have* to talk to can be a challenge, so moving beyond that is difficult to imagine. The most effective leaders do, however. They build a network of relationships outside their business, and even outside their industry, because they're curious about what's out there. They want to anticipate what's around the bend and beyond. They wonder what opportunities are available and what might get in the way. They also think about which companies they might partner with and which ones represent the biggest threats.

These considerations should be part of every leader's thought process, especially if you're a CEO. Thinking about them helps you move outside your own world and holistically expand your thinking to see your business from the perspectives of people on other continents, in other industries, on opposite teams, and in intersecting areas like government or academia. Not only does this provide you with the information you need to make sure you're not operating with blinders on, but it can inspire you to define an unimagined future for your company, division, or product line. When you let diverse relationships in, you never know where the path will lead. One of our favorite illustrations of this tenet involves Henry Ford and Thomas Edison.

As a young man on his father's farm in Dearborn, Michigan, Ford had followed Thomas Edison's career with much admiration. So when, at the age of fifteen, he left farm life and moved to Detroit, it seemed only natural that he should take a job at the Edison Illuminating Company. Starting out as a machinist, he soon worked his way up to chief engineer.

As the story goes, one year Ford's boss, Alex Dow, asked Ford to go with him to a company-sponsored convention in Manhattan Beach, New York. The guest of honor at the evening's opening banquet was none other than Edison himself. Knowing Ford's fascination with the inventor, Dow pointed Ford out to Edison, telling him, "There's a young fellow who has made a gas car." Over the course of the evening, Edison asked young Ford a host of questions, and when the interview was over, the older inventor emphasized his admiration by banging his fist down on the table. "Young man," he said, "that's the thing! You have it! Your car is self-contained and carries its own power plant!"

Years later, Ford, reflecting on this first meeting, said in a newspaper interview, "That bang on the table was worth worlds to me. No man up to then had given me any encouragement. I had hoped that I was headed right. Sometimes I knew that I was, sometimes I only wondered, but here, all at once and out of a clear sky, the greatest inventive genius in the world had given me complete approval. The man who knew most about electricity in the world had said that for the purpose, my gas motor was better than any electric motor could be."[1]

Ford never forgot those words of encouragement and the confidence they gave him to envision a future filled with affordable automobiles. When he became a wealthy industrialist, Ford joined Edison in many technical and scientific projects, and the two became lifelong friends. Over time, their network included

John Burroughs, naturalist Luther Burbank, Harvey Firestone, and occasionally President Warren G. Harding.[2] Who knows how the future was shaped on the camping trips the group enjoyed—but you can be sure it was.

To help you determine the breadth and depth of your network and how far you've extended the horizon for your team and your business, we challenge you to answer the following questions. If you can only answer a few, it's a good bet that your view is not broad enough to completely achieve your organization's fullest future potential.

1. Do you have external partners to assist with current or future strategic business needs (such as technology or product development)?
2. Do you know the most talented people in your industry but outside your company?
3. Do you regularly build personal relationships with customers? What about suppliers? Or Wall Street?
4. Do you find ways to work with a broad range of leaders both inside and outside your company? Do they include your competitors?
5. Do you understand the need for global relationships with governments and regulatory agencies on multiple continents? With how many countries do you have those kinds of relationships?

As you answered these questions, you may have wondered how you could possibly build so many relationships yourself. It doesn't happen overnight, and it may be that the connections come through other people on your team, and you only interact directly once in a while. That's fine.

The key here is to be learning and growing constantly by maintaining broad interactions and using everyone to develop new insights about opportunities and roadblocks today, tomorrow, or the next day. Find a way to hold yourself accountable for progress in building these relationships. Because it's not easy and the time it takes is limited, it's important to close the feedback loop with someone to whom you need to report progress. This could be a board member, a team member, or an outside coach who has your permission to hold you accountable. You just never know how important an inadvertent comment or an inspirational idea from these relationships might become. Someone out there might be *your* Thomas Edison. Without this broad exposure to keep you on top of your A-game, you might end up seeing only the individual trees in your forest. That would be a shame, because as we've come to learn, seeing—or more accurately, imagining—both the forest *and* the trees is one of the most important skills of the innovation leader.

One Whole Brain Is Better than a Dozen Half Brains

Scientists have known for a long time that the human brain consists of two parts: the left brain, which thinks in a verbal, organized, and analytical way; and the right brain, which is creative, nonverbal, or image based. The choice of which brain is in control of the day-to-day functions in our lives is what forges our personality and determines our character. For a long time, people believed that being left-brain dominant or right-brain dominant was something to which we were predisposed. In truth, it's more a matter of training.

Experiments show that most children rank as highly creative (right brain) before entering school. But because our educational system places a higher value on left-brain skills such as math, science, and language than it does on drawing or using imagination, only 10 percent of these same children rank as highly creative by age seven. By the time they're adults, a high level of creativity remains in only 2 percent of the population.[3]

Think about it. While innovation at its core is about creating something unique, we're trained to shut down the part of our brain that creates. Once we enter the corporate world, the left brain is valued even more. Processes, metrics, rules, economics, and bottom lines are all left-brain areas. Environments that put people in identical cubicles, force conformity, and forbid any type of personal expression in their space or personal appearance are all left brain. That's what we reward, so that's what we get: order, predictable outcomes, results that can be reduced to numbers—in short, control. That same order and conformity is also valued in society, so it's hard to escape even when we slip out of our work clothes and into our jeans. No wonder true innovation and true innovation leadership are so hard to come by.

But what if it were different? What if we gave the left brain a break and let the right brain in on a little of the action? Or better yet, what if, like Leonardo da Vinci, we used our whole brain? What could we accomplish?

As we look back on our careers and the people we've interviewed, we realize that some of the most successful leaders, whether they realize it or not, are able to cross between hemispheres and integrate their analytical and creative functions to bring about amazing innovations.

Think of this whole-brain orientation as creating an innovation flow that utilizes both sides of your brain. Sometimes the left will dominate and sometimes the right, but overall, you are creating a flow of thinking and decision making that cuts down the middle, creating an innovation flow that ensures you get the best from both sides of your brain. Depending on which type of innovation you are working on, you will inevitably lean more toward one side than the other. As illustrated in the following charts, Operational and Marketplace Innovation tend toward a left-brain orientation, whereas Transformational Innovation requires a strong right-brain orientation. Category Innovation straddles the fence. All four types of innovation benefit from whole-brain thinking and the innovation flow it creates.

FIGURE 6.1 Category/Operational/Marketplace Innovation

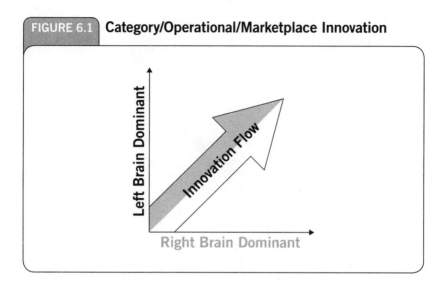

FIGURE 6.2 Transformational Innovation

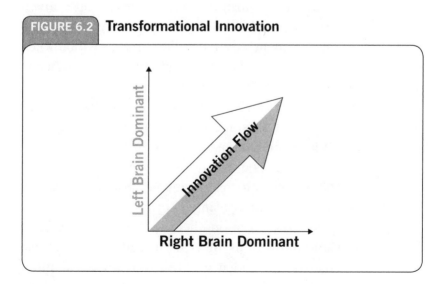

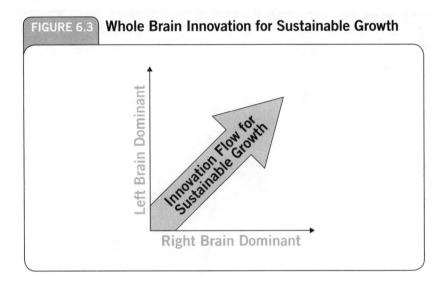

FIGURE 6.3 Whole Brain Innovation for Sustainable Growth

Take Michael Dell. In Chapter 1, we talked about the young upstart who took down IBM's personal computer business by moving his left-brain organizational skills into a right-brained vision. Unfortunately, much like Henry Ford, Dell got caught up in the left-brain-dominant world and didn't pay attention when companies like Apple and Hewlett-Packard were introducing colors and transparent shells that engaged consumers' imaginations. Today, Dell is fighting back with innovations like the Dell Streak, a device that falls somewhere between a smartphone and the iPad. Where this offering will land in the so-called tablet wars is yet to be seen, but what's important is that the company is back in the innovation game and not just playing follow the left-brained leader and focusing on price.

The ability to move from one hemisphere to the other in integrated, whole-brain thinking is what leads to sustainable innovation. You can see evidence of this in many of the innovators we've talked about, such as Steve Jobs, whose skills include connecting the dots between technology and consumer desires—a decidedly whole-brain function. A. G. Lafley shows cross-hemisphere agility in a different way, by being able to marry big-picture strategy and vision to operational prowess. Anne Mulcahy, retired chairman of Xerox; Nintendo's Satoru Iwata; and FedEx's Fred Smith—they all fall into this category as well. While each of these leaders differs considerably in management style, each has innovated their company to financial stability and growth over the past decade. It's not too far-fetched to believe that being whole-brain innovators is the link that connects them.

If you're going to be a great leader, you need to break through half-brain thinking. Remember the research that said creativity was *trained* out of children? That means it can be *trained* back in. Several works on the subject are available if you want to explore this idea further. The gist of restoring cross-brain functioning is that first you have to disengage the dominant half of your brain in order to engage the side you normally suppress. See if you recognize yourself in either of the following descriptions. It's not better to be one or the other; we are who we are. The point is to recognize your thinking pattern so you can engage the other hemisphere.

TABLE 6.2 Whole-Brain Innovation Leadership Characteristics— Using Both Sides, Who Are You?

LEFT-BRAIN CHARACTERISTICS	RIGHT-BRAIN CHARACTERISTICS
Logical	Emotional
Detail oriented	"Big-picture" oriented
Ruled by facts	Ruled by imagination
Comfortable with words and language	Comfortable with symbols and images
Focused on the present and past	Focused on the present and future

continued

| TABLE 6.2 | Whole-Brain Innovation Leadership Characteristics— Using Both Sides, Who Are You? *continued* |

LEFT-BRAIN CHARACTERISTICS	RIGHT-BRAIN CHARACTERISTICS
Applicable to math and science	Applicable to philosophy and religion
Able to comprehend	Able to "get it" (meanings)
Knowledge based	Belief based
Analytical	Conceptual
Good at order and patterns	Good at spatial perception
Can define things that are already created	Able to create new functions or systems
Reality based	Fantasy based
Able to form strategies	Able to present possibilities
Practical	Impetuous
Safe	Willing to take risks

The left side of your brain controls verbal ability, attention to detail, and reasoning. Left-brain-dominant people are good at communicating and persuading others. If you're left-brained, you are likely good at math and logic. Your desk tends to be neat and your day organized, and lists make you happy. Some say left-brainers prefer dogs over cats, reading over music, the quiet of the country over the activity and noise of a city, and logic over intuition.

The right side of your brain is all about creativity and flexibility. Daring and intuitive, right-brain people see the world in their own unique way. If you're right-brain dominant, you likely have a talent for creative writing and art. Your right brain pre-fers daydreaming, philosophy, and sports. You use your hands when you talk, and taking risks is not just okay, it's fun. Some say right-brainers get their best ideas when lying down or, if that's not possible, by getting up and moving around. Sitting up straight in a chair for long periods of time in a static space drives them nuts.

If you see yourself in both hemispheres, you're probably at least on your way to being a whole-brain thinker, which is where we all want to be. To get there, you need to exercise the part of your brain with which you're least comfortable. In other words, right-brain dominants need to exercise their left brain and vice versa. This can be as simple as changing some routines, like combing your hair or picking things up with your left hand (or your right one if you're a southpaw). If you're left-brain domi-nant, try closing your eyes when you're on an airplane or riding in a car and let your senses take in the sounds, smells, and feel of the environment; imagine what you're "seeing." When you have a problem, visualize a solution.

Physicality also disengages the left brain. Going for a walk, playing a regular game of golf or squash, dancing spontane-ously, exercising, tossing a ball, or crumbling up wads of paper and trying to make two points with a wastebasket free throw all work. Whatever helps you let go, gets you out of a rut, or relaxes you is all part of cross-training your brain.

If you're a right-brainer, you need to add some structure to your life to engage your left brain. In addition to changing up which hand you do things with, try making lists, either of what you need to do at the beginning of the day or what you accomplished at the end of the day. Play word games or solve crossword puzzles, both very left-brain activities. Take notes in a meeting and number action items or star important points. On an airplane, don't close your eyes and imagine; keep them open and take in details. Right-brain people tend to be big-picture thinkers, so training your brain to appreciate fine details will help you use your whole brain.

Once you know your dominant thinking style, you'll be better equipped to understand how you filter the way you see the world and thus how you solve problems, make decisions, and communicate. Exceptional leaders know themselves, their strengths and weaknesses, and their capabilities and limitations, even when it comes to thinking style. Being tuned in to this style also helps you understand your people—what comes naturally to them, what motivates them, and how to get their buy-in. Knowing what thinking style you and your people gravitate toward is the starting place for integrating the two hemispheres into whole-brain thinking.

As a leader, cross-training your brain for whole-brain innovation and encouraging others to do the same can be one of your greatest assets. The greater the engagement of both the right and the left sides of your brain, the broader the scope of innovation for you and your company. Not only can you envision more possibilities this way, you'll also be able to sustain innovation across the levels for a longer period of time. You'll be an artist, not just a painter.

Leadership Sustainability— The Beauty of a Balanced Life

We've talked a lot about what it takes to become an extraordinary leader of innovation. Now we'd like to talk about how you build a life that sustains those capabilities. While many leaders have the capabilities and characteristics we've talked about, they also have vulnerabilities and trials that are taxing. Whether we like to admit it or not, our performance is impaired when we don't recharge our batteries. Since the time of Plato, we've known that human beings operate on four levels: physical, intellectual, emotional, and spiritual.[4] Keeping a balance on all levels keeps you in shape for peak performance. How you do that depends on what "feeds" you.

Fabrizio Freda, president and chief executive officer of The Estée Lauder Companies, is admired as a strong leader of innovation. He takes his job very seriously, but he also knows that downtime is important to his success as a leader. Freda is religious about his commitment to living a balanced life and sets priorities to make sure it happens. "My first priority is always my family," he says. "I don't let my work overshadow them. When I'm home, I make sure I have a good amount of time to devote to them. At work, I think one of my most important jobs is thinking strategically, so I schedule regular breaks to stay fresh and spend at least twenty-five minutes a day in strategy mode."

Similarly, Mike McCallister, chairman, chief executive officer, and president of health care innovator Humana, uses the weekends to help himself rejuvenate and give his mind a breather from the workweek's hard-core business focus. He finds that he's able to think more clearly and bring more of himself to the job when he takes a break to refresh and restore.

All of us need to find our own way to balance life and make sure we're surrounded by things that make us happy and energized. For some, it's golf; for others, it might be hiking, fishing, music, or gourmet cooking. Reading for pleasure or exercising can also push your reset button, as can volunteering, spending time with friends, camping, or going on a romantic getaway or spiritual retreat. Whatever brings balance to your life, make sure it's something you commit to on a regular basis. Staying fresh, passionate, and on top of your game is extremely important to driving innovation.

When we live too much in our job and let the rest of our life stagnate, it not only robs us of energy physically, emotionally and spiritually, it actually narrows the life experiences that help us be the well-rounded, whole-brain thinkers we strive to be. And while we've often said innovation is the responsibility of top leadership, being responsible doesn't mean you have to go it alone. In fact, no matter where you are in the leadership chain, the support of others helps you survive and thrive. After all, the life balance you model is what will likely be reflected by your organization. As leaders, we all have a responsibility both to take care of ourselves and to enhance the opportunities and well-being of our team members. Not only is it the responsible thing to do, it's the smart thing to do.

In the next chapter, we'll drill down on the specific leadership capabilities essential for the four levels of innovation. In the process of learning about who you are and what and who you need on your team, you'll undoubtedly find out what type of innovation best suits your personal leadership style as well. The more layers of the innovation onion you peel, the closer you get to your goal of creating sustainable growth.

CHAPTER 7

Leadership Personalities

The Right Stuff

In order to strike a balance between the day-to-day
operational needs of the company and an innovation
agenda, you have to understand that the people
on both sides are as different as night and day.

—MIKE MCCALLISTER, CHAIRMAN, CEO, AND PRESIDENT, HUMANA

n his book *Winning,* Jack Welch wrote that when picking
a leader for a commodity business, he chose the obsessive
type who was a "master of discipline," but when he picked
a CEO for an innovative and risky business, he chose a
person who "hated the nuts and bolts" but had the "guts
and vision to place the big bets." Understanding how remarkably different these types are and how to use a person's natural
talents was one of Welch's most important skills. By matching
personalities to each function and business, he was able to build
high-performance teams.

When it comes to innovation, developing that same level of
skill should be at the top of every leader's list. The most effective

companies have an integrated approach in which all four levels of innovation are constantly in play. For this reason, it's important not only to understand which level is right for each division and function, but to know which personality can deliver that innovation most effectively. The person best suited to lead a company through an industry-defining breakthrough is rarely the same one who can brilliantly launch it to market. Each job requires different talents, a different personality, and a different leadership style to maximize potential.

Equally as important as having the right personality for the job is providing the right environment for that leader to succeed. Think about it. You wouldn't use a Formula One racing car to explore the rugged Australian outback, nor would you drop a Hummer onto an Indy 500 track. Both are great performers in the right environment, but driven out of their element, the results can be disastrous.

In the last chapter, we looked at the general capabilities and characteristics of top executives of innovation. In this chapter, we'll peel the onion even more and look at leadership profiles as they relate to the four types of innovation. To help you zero in on the perfect match, we've constructed profiles that correspond with each level. These not only define individual characteristics and personality traits, but they also show what typically motivates the leader, what the culture for each type of innovation needs to be, and perhaps most significant, what the organization needs to give them to be successful.

These profiles aren't meant to pigeonhole or label people; they're meant to be a guide to help you recognize fit and capabilities. As we talk about the different personalities, think about the people around you. Are they suited for the work they're asked to do? Are you? As you read and reflect, you may think of other personal characteristics that typify innovation leaders you've had experience with in each of the innovation categories defined. If so, note them at the appropriate levels for future reference. It's important to begin to see people in terms of their innovation potential and your company in terms of both depth and reach of talent. When you have the right people in the right jobs focused on innovation throughout the company, the mix works like magic.

The Four Leadership Types

If you've ever wondered why some people walk into a project or new position and take over like they've always been there and others never seem to get comfortable, it's likely a matter of fit. While talented people tend to get the job done, there's a huge difference between knowing what to do intellectually and feeling it intuitively. When it comes naturally, creativity flows more easily, and less energy is spent on thinking about what to do.

Just as important as feeling right for the job is working in a culture that nurtures your innovative nature instead of hindering it. For example, those involved in Operational Innovation might feel secure enough to make suggestions that could eliminate their job, knowing the company would find another spot for them; however, it could just as easily be an everyone-for-themselves situation. Does a category innovator have the trust and freedom to make funding decisions without jumping through countless hoops, or is he or she questioned at every turn?

Understanding what motivates, activates, and enables people for each innovation culture is central to creating an environment of growth. Frankly, this is something few companies do well. Most cultures are "one size fits all." They fail to recognize that innovation is inherently different from the day-to-day business of the company and, as such, needs different considerations and a variety of personality types. You wouldn't weave a tapestry with only one color of thread. Neither can you build an innovation organization with only one kind of leader. So let's meet our master weavers.

The Transformational Leader

When you dissect Transformational Innovation, at its center is one person—at the most, two or three—who can't rest until he or she finds the sought-after solution. At their core, transformational leaders are highly creative and have the ability to see things in a way that few others can. It's no surprise then that this leader has a unique profile that's as rare as Transformational Innovation itself.

What makes these leaders tick are possibilities—the more, the better. Often impatient, persistent, committed, and visionary, they're not afraid of failure or what others might see as setbacks. On the contrary, they're as committed to learning from mistakes or failures as they are to successes, because these lessons are the road signs that ultimately lead them to the prize.

TABLE 7.1 The Transformational Leader

PERSONAL CHARACTERISTICS	PRIMARY MOTIVATORS
Ability to be a game changer, to think outside the box and see what others don't	Causes bigger than self
Strong-minded and fiercely independent, not afraid of failure en route to success	Unbridled curiosity
Technically insightful and intuitive	The possibility of discovery and invention
Apolitical, not willing to finesse things to play the game	
Knowledgeable about the subject matter being addressed	
Determined to succeed	
Passionate in commitment to what he/she believes possible	

The excitement these leaders feel comes from fueling innovations that shape our future. That's their reward. They're not looking for the limelight, they don't necessarily want to build empires, and they aren't motivated by the prospect of enormous wealth. They want to change the world. What they love most and do best is create, not just products but possibilities. Innovation on a grand scale is in their blood.

There probably isn't a better example of this profile type than Dean Kamen, founder and chief executive officer of DEKA. A self-taught physicist and multimillionaire entrepreneur, most of Kamen's wealth stems from inventing things he thought *should* exist rather than things market research said *could* exist. That he does so with regularity and singular purpose puts him in the same league as Thomas Edison, another transformational

IDEAL CULTURE	WHAT THE ORGANIZATION NEEDS TO PROVIDE
Climate of empowerment Focus on discovery Freedom to fail Trust oriented	Space to be creative away from headquarters Empowerment to focus, explore, and discover without corporate encumbrances Measures of success based on achieving milestones on the journey, not traditional bottom-line metrics A long-term horizon

personality. Curious, committed, and respected for finding his motivation and reward in changing lives, Kamen is often called on to take up causes others would never attempt.

In 2005, Defense Advanced Research Projects Agency (DARPA) director Tony Tether and Revolutionizing Prosthetics program manager Colonel Geoffrey Ling approached Kamen, saying that so far sixteen hundred young soldiers had come back from war missing an arm, sometimes two. Their request was for him to make an artificial limb weighing less than nine pounds that someone could use to pick up and eat a grape without crushing it.[1] Kamen says he thought they were crazy "in the good kind of way."

There was no financial incentive to create a next-generation prosthetic arm. The research and development costs were enormous. Unless DARPA funded it, no private company would take such a risk for such a comparatively small market (in the Americas, about six thousand people require arm prostheses each year). Despite every reason not to undertake the project, Kamen spent a few weeks traveling around the country and interviewing patients, doctors, and researchers to get an idea of the current technology. He was astonished by the difference between the current leg and arm prostheses. "Prosthetic legs are in the twenty-first century," he says. "With prosthetic arms, we're in the Flintstones era."

It was intriguing, but the last thing he needed was another mission. He was already working on portable electricity and purifying water for developing nations, a project he believes could wipe out 50 percent of the world's diseases. But even though he was already working day and night, he couldn't walk away. "My parents used to call me 'the human irritant,'" he remembers. "They said if I decided to do something, nothing would stop me unless I decided to stop. On this one, I couldn't stop." Instead, he and a team of twenty engineers set out to reinvent the prosthesis that had been much the same since the Civil War.

On the second floor of the mill complex that houses Kamen's company, DEKA Research and Development Corp, a 650-square-meter space was dedicated to realizing what has been dubbed the Luke arm, a prosthesis named for the remarkably lifelike prosthetic worn by Luke Skywalker in *Star Wars*. Just past the entrance is a life-sized Terminator figure missing its left arm; in its place is the same kind of harness that patients wear when testing the DEKA arm. It's there for inspiration. "What I ask of all my people is to see things without limitation and to imagine the impossible," notes Kamen. His philosophy of limitless thinking is part of the enormous success he and his team have had in turning out one Transformational Innovation after another faster than anyone could imagine.

The first prototype Luke arm was unveiled fifteen months after the initial DARPA visit and deemed very promising. The journey isn't over though. As the costly research and development phase moves into clinical trials, it's hoped that some company will take over the Luke arm and look for ways to manufacture it cost-effectively. In typical transformational fashion, bringing a product to market is of little interest to Kamen, which is why you wouldn't want him leading a global corporation. Even if he would take such a job (he wouldn't), the politics, accountability, and structure would drive him nuts. Self-proclaimed as impatient to a fault, compulsive, obsessive, unreasonable, and demanding, he is not the type to charm a board of directors. But if you ask him to develop a product for you, he'll keep working and working and working. He says he won't stop until everyone in the world has access to clean water, and he means it.

His other passion is an idea that may be far-fetched even for him: turning engineers and inventors into pop-culture superstars. Operating through a nonprofit outfit called FIRST

(For Inspiration and Recognition of Science and Technology), Kamen works to encourage kids to pursue careers as scientists, engineers, and big thinkers. Lots of people talk about helping to foster kids into these careers, but to Kamen, it's a holy crusade. He sincerely believes he can reprioritize society to value inventors the way it currently values athletes. "Our culture celebrates many different kinds of celebrity, especially in sports," he says. "You have teenagers thinking they're going to make millions as NBA stars when that's not realistic for even 1 percent of them. Becoming a scientist or an engineer is." Now in its twenty-first year, the organization involves more than thirty-five hundred corporations in its mission. Among them are several companies that understand, as Kamen does, the importance of Transformational Innovation and have made a commitment to nurturing it in a special environment.

Thought of as "discovery centers," companies like General Electric, Procter & Gamble, and IBM have created rarified cultures to protect emerging ideas from the metrics of less risky innovation. Without this protection, a lot of breakthroughs would die. In fact, GE's Jeffrey Immelt works directly with transformational leaders to make sure they don't get mired in the same quarterly expectations as the rest of the business.

"We know our people need an environment that isn't bogged down by bureaucracy," explains Mark Little, GE's senior vice president and director of research centers. "The people here are the ones who will uncover new forms of energy, cures for cancer, or new ways to diagnose disease and treat it proactively. They need the room to be curious and the freedom to explore." To give them that room, GE's research centers are located far from the hubbub of its corporate locations, where there are an abundance of controls. "Process stifles innovation," says Beth Comstock, GE's senior vice president and chief marketing officer. "We have so many processes at GE, and while that's necessary in a company this large, too much kills innovation. We will never be as nimble and unstructured as a company like DEKA, but we've worked hard to make incubation part of our DNA, both internally and with our innovation partners. It's how we protect the big ideas from destruction before they have the chance to breathe."

That, in a nutshell, is the essence of both the transformational personality and the culture needed to nurture it—room to breathe and the independence and autonomy to bring big ideas to life.

The Category Leader

Unlike the more solitary transformational leader, this individual is a builder and thrives on creating growth opportunities, not just for the company, but for individuals as well. This is the person who can take in the 35,000-foot view, see the dots on the map formed by Transformational Innovations like the Internet, and build entire industries where none existed. What's more, this leader has the ability to spot opportunity before it's registered on anyone else's radar.

These people also value knowledge and progressive thinking and can utilize both to create new ideas in their chosen industry. They "know what they know" and are not likely to change their minds unless they see the value of change for themselves. Fond of argument and debate, they use both as a learning/growing exercise, because it helps them see both sides of an issue and decide for themselves what's best or right.

Boards, CEOs and other leaders usually relate well to the category personality, not only because he or she possesses an uncanny ability to influence others, but also because this person is more focused on business achievement than personal achievement. The best category leaders are also very team focused and get pleasure from helping others grow and develop. They like

TABLE 7.2	The Category Leader	
PERSONAL CHARACTERISTICS		**PRIMARY MOTIVATORS**
Highly innovative, creative, sees trends and patterns easily		Achieving business success
Business savvy		Building/creating growth opportunities
Excellent impact and influencing skills		
Decisive and willing to take deliberate risks		Developing people
Ability to leverage a network of people and resources		Winning together with those around them, internal and external to the company
Desire to move quickly, often impatient with politics		

to win on a big scale for everyone. It's what motivates them and how they measure their own success. They are often seen as entrepreneurial and comfortable with risk.

While it's true they're most effective when given the freedom to operate like business owners, they thrive in an organization because it gives them the opportunity and resources to create something memorable. Whether they're building a new business or a great team, this characteristic is core to category leaders. Thus, it makes sense that such leaders like to be in a collaborative environment, one that lets them work with others across functional areas. Just because they like team spirit, however, doesn't mean they're shy about making decisions. This is a "head coach" personality with a strong level of self-confidence and the ability to take risks. This person has a real gift for connecting the dots with power and certainty, so it doesn't work well if he or she has to jump through hoops for funding approval. If trusted

IDEAL CULTURE	WHAT THE ORGANIZATION NEEDS TO PROVIDE
Focused on the market	Focus on growth
Insights guide the destination	Investment consistent with priorities
Focused on delivery and plays to win	Freedom to fail in order to win big
Collaborative, with cross-functional teams	Market-focused vision
Climate of empowerment	Rewards for creating value
Operates like a business owner	

to do the right thing and make the right decisions, true category leaders do what's best for the company.

The bottom line here is ownership, self-confidence, and trust that if you take care of the company, the company will take care of you. When Bilal was at Kraft, he saw the power of this type of leadership firsthand, but it didn't start out that way.

"In the early nineties, the company's cheese division had been having trouble getting new products over the line and was struggling to produce market share and revenue growth," he recalls. "In several cases, even when we had the right products, our launches were disjointed. One department would do one thing and another one something else without coordination, so we could never get solid traction in the marketplace."

It was purely a cultural problem. Instead of cross-functional teams that worked collaboratively to run the business, the company had functional silos. When the business won on volume, share and profit lost out, and when it won on profit, volume and share didn't line up. What needed to happen was "trifecta" performance—or superior outcomes on all three measures. "We had good category leaders," notes Bilal. "But the culture wasn't supporting them. By giving category teams a sense of ownership in aggressively driving their business, that changed."

Once there was profit-and-loss accountability with full cross-functional teams, Kraft could set both short- and long-term agendas for each category. This played into a primary motivator for category personalities—to see the company and its teams succeed. Now each team was responsible for the quality of the category as well as for delivering the upside market potential. The resulting environment was consumer and retail customer focused and growth driven. "There was tremendous satisfaction from seeing real growth," says Bilal. Both category teams in which he was involved repeatedly won the coveted Chairman's Award for outstanding performance in growing volume, share, and profit. The trifecta.

In addition to the business results, teams learned to count on and trust each other and to leverage strengths and cover constraints. Bilal learned to think way beyond his functional research expertise as a business leader, as did each of the other functional leaders. A level of caring also developed between team members that, in many cases, has continued to this day, decades later. What this cross-functional team tapped into was the strength of the category personality and culture—insight, ownership, and collaboration.

The Marketplace Leader

While the category leader might be thought of as the head coach, the marketplace leader may be described as the quarterback—the one who executes the plays. The world of the marketplace leader is competitive, exciting, and more focused on the present than either of his or her counterparts in Transformational or Category Innovation. This is the person you want if you're launching line extensions; revitalizing brands; or finding unique ways to reach the market or understand customers, consumers, and competitors. This is also the profile where we start moving toward more structure. Marketplace leaders perform best when they know the game plan and what their role in it is.

As befits their responsibility in reading the market, marketplace types are naturally in tune with and sensitive to others' feelings, moods, and attitudes. They are the human equivalent of a mood ring. They usually relate well to others and express themselves easily. Marketplace leaders love to share ideas and bring clarity to complex situations; they are often enthusiastic and can spontaneously adapt to changing situations. Because of their communication skills and ability to read people, they're also skilled negotiators. Whatever task they're given, the key to productivity is using their ability to communicate, clarify, and motivate others.

Hasbro, a company we talked about in Chapter 5, was looking to move from a product orientation to a brand focus with several of its lines, including Nerf. Originally, the category had been developed as a new kind of soft toy. People liked it, but after decades of the same message, most people, including Jane, thought of it as an "old-line" brand. At least until her twelve-year-old son and his friends started clamoring for multiple new types of Nerf blasters. Why was the old toy suddenly appealing again? The answer is Marketplace Innovation and a leader who understood how to create an environment where fresh ideas turned into fresh products.

The category needed to be revived, and since this type of innovation is all about bringing new iterations to life and finding inventive ways to reach the market, Brian Goldner, the

| TABLE 7.3 | The Marketplace Leader |

PERSONAL CHARACTERISTICS	PRIMARY MOTIVATORS
Preference for boundaries and frameworks	Healthy competition
Strong in project management	Endorsement by superiors
Process oriented and metric focused	Sales and customer satisfaction
Excellent people skills	Affiliation with others— recharges by being with people
Thinking in terms of features and benefits	
Politically savvy and good at motivating	

company's president and CEO, set out to motivate and excite his team. His first order of business was to put clear milestones in place. First on the list was reigniting the passion of the consumer. Talks with customers revealed that the real appeal of Nerf toys was the fact that kids could safely play outdoor games inside without moms getting nervous. These toys didn't break lamps or knock over knickknacks. Boys could go to war with Nerf swords and no one would get hurt. Armed with this insight from marketing, the design team was able to pair revenue upside with existing technology. This type of cross-fertilization is a hallmark of the Marketplace Innovation. Working together, the Nerf team tapped into a whole new generation of kids by essentially moving away from the mind-set of manufacturing a toy toward one of delivering play. And the company did deliver—ahead of schedule—growing this somewhat mature category from $30 million to $400 million.

This wasn't the first home run for Goldner on the marketplace level. Before becoming CEO at Hasbro, he served as the

IDEAL CULTURE	WHAT THE ORGANIZATION NEEDS TO PROVIDE
Based on a clear business strategy and execution plan	Commitment to business plans
	Cross-functional alignment
Can-do atmosphere	Appropriate resources
Matrix driven	Incentives for success and celebration of achievements
Structured and clearly defined	
Financially focused	Focus on keeping categories growing
Speed in decision making and execution operations	

head of North American operations for rival toy maker Bandai. There his creativity, marketing savvy, and innovative style resulted in numerous new product introductions and profitable partnerships for the Bandai family. Goldner's achievements included a 15 percent sales increase for its Power Rangers line and a launch hit with Bandai's Yomega yo-yos, which captured more than 55 percent of dollar share in its first year on the market.[2] These successes helped him hone his innovation style even further. In fact, the marketplace level is one of the best training and proving grounds for future category leaders. In the right culture, one that is focused on execution and managing expectations, there's a lot of room for growth. It's here that people who appreciate deadlines, budgets, and commitments to colleagues thrive. The culture for Marketplace Innovation should also honor the constant juggling of conflicting internal and external priorities, so it's important to provide this leader with recognition for his or her achievements. Getting the Marketplace Innovation culture right is a very profitable proposition.

The Operational Leader

Of all the leadership personalities, operational leaders are the perfectionists of the group. They are intelligent, sensible, and correct. They are detail oriented, conscientious, and systematic. They like to plan ahead and live by facts and logic. Operational leaders usually dislike spontaneity and carelessness, and they are often intolerant of anything that does not stem from what they consider to be rational thought.

These are inside people. They like working in a community, but it's more about being on a continuous learning path than a need for social connection. Applying formulas and financial aspects, putting things together, and solving tough problems are a particular joy for these personalities when given the right environment.

TABLE 7.4 The Operational Leader

PERSONAL CHARACTERISTICS	PRIMARY MOTIVATORS
Focused on cost (productivity is king)	Creating order out of chaos (greatest joy)
Organized, seeing order and process easily	Achievement of measurable goals
Detail oriented	Acknowledgement of contribution by peers and superiors
Risk averse	A sense of community
Disinclined to large-scale change	
Thinks in terms of black or white, uncomfortable with gray	

In work relationships, they can have trouble letting go of the need to be right unless they're working with others to solve a complex problem. These leaders are happiest working with people who can appreciate their razor-sharp mind and understand their need for alone time. The best praise for them is acknowledgement of their achievement by peers and superiors. An operational leader at the helm of the company feels rewarded by seeing the organization run efficiently and at peak performance. Depending on the life cycle of the company, this leader may be just what the doctor ordered, especially if he or she is surrounded with the right mix of innovation leaders.

Because cost is king and productivity reigns in Operational Innovation, the culture deals well with clear goals and established metrics for evaluating achievements. This is an

IDEAL CULTURE	WHAT THE ORGANIZATION NEEDS TO PROVIDE
Deals well with "doers"	Orientation and investment in best practices
Commits to staff training and development	
Sets clear deliverables and is focused on execution of the plan	Recognition of community, individual accomplishments, and team achievements
Thinks about everything in terms of efficiency and effectiveness	Focus on continuous education and improvement
Clarifies roles; sets goals and metrics by which to evaluate achievement of goals	Reinforcement of operating guidelines

environment that needs to nurture players who are highly dependable and "follow the rules." Black-and-white values dominate the operational group, and a sense of community is important to reinforce their values.

Quality and productivity are also major components of the operational culture, and because it's so metric focused, people need to know what defines success. For example, if you define cost cutting as the measure of success, that will immediately become the cultural driver—not innovation. In fact, if cost cutting is what is requested, innovation will seem too risky, because another hallmark of the operational culture is the need for a significant level of safety and predictability. Where innovation is concerned, the transformational leader asks, "Why not?" and the operational leader asks, "Why?" Any course of action needs to make sense. Repeatability and value for predictable outcomes are important attributes in this culture, and when that's the motivator, there's no limit to what the operational personality can do.

When Bilal was at Frito Lay, he worked with a number of outstanding Operational Innovation leaders who taught him how valuable this type of innovation can be. These leaders built their culture around playing to win and producing the lowest-cost product with the highest quality. They set up healthy competition among their plants to achieve what most thought were impossible goals. By developing a way to share key capabilities with a new, fast-adoption mentality, they achieved every one.

Culturally, they did something quite innovative when they created and adopted a no debate process. "No debate" meant that any capability that was proven in another plant would be adopted without argument by other plants unless they could come up with an idea that surpassed the proven one. This approach quickly built rapport and focused the plants on winning together versus the former "not invented here" mentality that fostered win-lose competition.

In many cases, the new proven capabilities enabled the consolidation of plants. The teams were actually supportive of these moves at the expense of their then-current jobs, because they knew there was a mutual commitment between them and the company. If they did the right thing for the company, they knew the company would do the right thing for them.

This culture provided the security necessary to help them feel confident that their unique capabilities would make it possible for Frito Lay to move them into new roles that used their skills. This is the power of a healthy Operational Innovation culture. It can be defined in three words: efficiency, effectiveness, and teamwork.

The Magic Mix

Just as important as having the right people in the right job is having enough of them. Throughout Part 1, we talked about the necessity of being continually engaged in multiple levels of innovation. You can't rely on just one if you want sustainable growth. It stands to reason then that you need a steward for each type of innovation in the leadership ranks. But just as there is no one profile that's best suited to a CEO, there is no prescribed mix of leaders to guarantee innovation success. What's important is that all the bases are covered to keep multiple levels of innovation flowing. To do this, a leader needs to find that unique balance of team support that complements and completes his or her strengths and is attuned to the life cycle of the company. When the right people are in the right place at the right time, the mix can work like magic, something Burberry found out with the teaming of CEO Angela Ahrendts and chief creative officer Christopher Bailey.

When we introduced this dynamic duo in the last chapter, we mentioned how they had often talked about what they would do if they were running the show. They had big dreams, and when they were given the chance to realize those dreams, the results were nothing less than mind-blowing.

Fashion Week is a notoriously elitist venture in which private shows are given for the most important buyers, clients, and press. The rest of the world has always had to wait to see what the next hot fashion trends will be. However, Ahrendts and Bailey wanted to change that in a spectacular way. Bailey proposed the first-ever live Internet broadcast of a global fashion show. It would be groundbreaking. It would be the envy of the industry. And it would take both Ahrendts's organizational genius and Bailey's transformational vision to pull it off.

Using a combination of technologies, they simultaneously live-streamed the event in normal 2D to online viewers and in nearly real 3D to screening rooms at five private sites in Paris, New York, Dubai, Tokyo, and Los Angeles. "The 3D technology brings our global audience into the London show space, allowing them to see the colors and fabrics, to hear the music, and to be a part of that moment when it all finally comes together," explains Bailey.

In addition to "being there," buyers around the world were offered the first live click-and-buy opportunity. As soon as they saw a piece they liked, they could press a button and the order was automatically forwarded to the manufacturer, with delivery promised within weeks. The commercial success of this idea was undeniable. Coupled with the efforts of other initiatives, the Burberry team posted record profits for the company.[3]

What Ahrendts and Bailey have is something every company covets—a dream team that can navigate innovation like a well-oiled machine. Building that team doesn't happen overnight though. It takes effort, focus, and an unflappable belief in what you're doing.

A. G. Lafley spent his entire career moving up Procter & Gamble's corporate ladder. For years he had been thinking about how to make the company relevant in the twenty-first century, when speed and agility would matter more than heft. His vision was to turn the internally focused culture into one in which consumer-centric innovation was the prime directive.

It was an ambitious vision for a 162-year-old company, but one that he believed was not only possible but critical to survival. Before he could act on his vision though, he had a few problems to deal with.

The 1990s had not been good to the aging conglomerate. The competition was beating it out left and right. The Swiffer duster was the only significant innovation it had had in fifteen years, and shareholders were unhappy. In 1999, the board sought salvation in Durk Jager, a veteran P&Ger, who was appointed CEO and tasked with turning the flailing company around.

Strong-willed and brash, Jager charged into office determined to dismantle P&G's insular culture and remake it from the bottom up. But instead of pushing the company to excel, his methods alienated employees and drove the stock price into the basement. It was a disaster. Within seventeen months, it was clear that Jager was not the right man for the job. On June 6, 2000, an unprecedented boardroom coup took place in Cincinnati. Jager was out. A. G. Lafley was in.[4]

While Lafley didn't fundamentally disagree with Jager's vision, he understood that things had moved too fast. This was a company that had always been resistant to change, especially the iron-fisted change Jager had introduced. Instead of taking the time and care to dissect the different types of businesses to see where they were in the innovation landscape and what would offer the best-integrated strategy, Jager had tried to ram through one new product after another. His handling of people hadn't been any better. He hadn't thoughtfully picked leaders who could make a difference and then trusted them to do the job; he'd demanded instant results. Change was needed, and the company had to become less conservative and make more bold moves. But instilling fear and expecting a brutal approach to make it successful had been an enormous miscalculation.

Lafley understood this, so his first priority was to restore morale and put an end to internal chaos. He set out to simplify things by letting people go back to what they knew best—the company's strongest brands. Relieved of the pressure to invent the "next big thing," at least for the moment, they could focus on Marketplace Innovations through packaging, marketing, and line extensions.

A proponent of "customer first" from the beginning, Lafley believed that baby care, the company's second largest division after laundry, was ripe for innovation but lacked the leadership to engage the consumer. As he put it, "The machine guys and the plant guys were running the show. . . . The machine was boss." In a bold move that passed over dozens of men with seniority, he selected Deb Henretta to take charge. Henretta, who had come up through the laundry division and had no experience in baby care, didn't care about how the machines worked. What mattered to her was first understanding the consumer and then making the machines work for her. Lafley was convinced she was the one for the job, but his decision wasn't popular. In fact, he had to take a step back and allow team members to make a case for their favorite candidates. He considered their choices seriously, but in the end, he still believed he'd made the right decision. He then explained his reasoning, and while there were still those who were unhappy, the resistance was neutralized.[5]

The CEO used this same approach of suitability for the job rather than seniority in building his teams throughout his tenure, ensuring that there was strong leadership at every level. He retained the promote-from-within policy P&G is known for, but he made it a point to weed out underperformers. In 2001, he started what is known as the Talent Portfolio, a blue book that contains the names of P&G's up-and-coming leaders. Each person is evaluated on financial and leadership abilities and compared to his or her peers. The book also contains lists of who is ready to be promoted next, who will be ready after the current assignment, and who will need more time. At any one time, there are at least three candidates for any major job, making it easier to create the synergistic leadership needed for an innovation culture.

To give his people more ideas to work with, Lafley also directly confronted the long-held notion that everything must be invented within P&G. He challenged his people to bring in half of the company's new products from the outside. This meant buying or supporting outside incubation of innovation when necessary. It also meant reaching out to former P&Gers through company support of an alumni network. By tapping into the vast experience of former employees, the company's external business development program created an avenue for partnering with alumni on innovative solutions. Lafley also set up a well-buffered innovation center whose job was to identify transformational product ideas and opportunities to reshape the business. Among the most surprising innovations to come out of the Lafley era was the Mr. Clean car wash franchise, which built off the megabrand cleaning product. In 2007, the company opened two test sites. Today, it's the largest car wash franchise in the country.[6]

When Lafley took over the reins, his goal was to bring P&G into the next century and open up the minds of more than 100,000 employees. It's not an overstatement to say that's exactly what he did. By turning the once-staid company into a hive of innovation, executing bold business deals, putting the right people in the right jobs, and fostering an absolute focus on the customer, P&G's sales doubled, profits quadrupled, and market value increased by more than $100 billion dollars.[7] But even with his remarkable success, Lafley says the transformation of P&G from conventional to innovative is no more than 10 percent complete. He believes building an innovative culture in old-style, big organizations takes at least a generation, even with the best of leadership. Time will tell if he's right.

In 2009, he turned the company over to the next generation. Now in the carefully chosen hands of Robert McDonald, it will experience a different style of leadership but one that Lafley thinks is just right for P&G as it faces today's greater cost pressures. "I'm a good operator," says Lafley. "I think he's a great operator."[8] That may be, but what's certain is that the new chief has had the best training anyone could hope for. P&G may still be going through growing pains, but Lafley's focus on developing a multifaceted leadership team and moving innovation outside the company and into the world has given McDonald a good foundation to build on.

His job now will be to keep the cultural change going and evolving, and he seems poised to do that. Building on Lafley's famous line "The customer is boss," McDonald charges his people with a greater vision: "Touch and improve more people's lives, in more parts of the world, more completely."[9] When someone suggests that's hard to do with shaving cream, McDonald tells the story of how feminine napkins are helping girls in sub-Saharan Africa get educated. Before they had access to them, girls were banned from school for one week a month. Now they're not. Developing markets like this currently make up 30 percent of P&G's sales and are core to its strategy. How fitting that a company that just a decade ago was determined to keep itself focused inward is now purposely reaching out. While some might call this miraculous, we say it was just a matter of having the right people in the right place at the right time.

PART 3

THE PAYOFF: ACTIVATING GROWTH

One of the simplest explanations we've heard about activating innovation is as follows: innovation is a team sport; you can't win solo. To realize the fruits of your innovation efforts, you have to have both your company (players) and your customers (fans) enthusiastically with you. Without both, you might as well stay home.

As innovation becomes more and more of a top priority in the corporate world, the need to address culture is reaching crisis proportions. Survey after survey shows that the single greatest barrier to innovation is the company itself. It isn't lack of ideas, lack of a process, or even determination of leadership; it's the team—or more precisely, the rules, attitudes, and very thought processes of the environment that's to blame.

Over the past two decades, corporate cultures have, more often than not, demanded a focus on cost cutting, outsourcing, and process excellence. While certainly not bad on their own, these decidedly left-brain dictates all but shut down the whole-brain thinking needed for innovation. What's more, when metrics based on financial performance rule, risk taking goes out the window. No one wants to be on the wrong end of the spreadsheet. And let's face it, it's much more comfortable to keep things as they are than to adapt to change. If the culture is wrong, however, it will derail the best efforts of an innovation strategy. If you're willing to fix it, it can give your company a shot at greatness.

We say "a shot" because the final judge of whether your innovation will pass or fail still lies with the customer. It's amazing how many companies, after spending millions of dollars developing an idea, fail at this juncture. They fail because of timing, poor insight, lack of agility, and sometimes just sheer arrogance. The prize belongs to whoever can engage, excite, and activate the customer, not only to want to follow that company, but to become its biggest fan. Just as there are ways to pull your team together, there are proven ways to catch the customer's eye, giving your innovation the best chance for adoption.

In the final chapters of *Breaking Away*, we will address both of these vital issues—activating your company and your customers to bring the real payoff of innovation (sustainable growth) home. First, we'll talk about attitude, respect, and how to create an environment where people both understand their role in innovation and want to be an integral part of it.

In the market activation chapter, we'll address the essential steps of customer engagement as well as examples of brilliant moves and unfortunate mishaps. We all make mistakes, but hopefully we can learn from them before they cost us a great product. Finally, in the last chapter, we will talk about one of the most important steps in making innovation part of your company DNA, and that's activating yourself. Innovation needs champions, and most often champions aren't born—they're made. With desire, dedication, and a determination to overcome whatever obstacles arise, that champion can be you.

CHAPTER 8

Activating
People

One for All and All for One

If you leave us our buildings and our brands but
take away our people, the company will fail.

**—RICHARD "RED" DEUPREE, CHIEF EXECUTIVE
OFFICER, PROCTER & GAMBLE, 1947[1]**

One of the greatest assets any company has, without a doubt, is its people. Yes, people—those elusive, sometimes puzzling, and often frustrating individuals who can either be your ticket to success or a dismal end of the road. When left to their own devices, people will sometimes play as a team, but more often, they're looking for their spot in the lifeboat. Given today's typical corporate culture, it's no wonder. In the last two decades, job security has essentially become an urban myth. With downsizing, rightsizing, and recession sizing, people have little incentive to care about the success of the company, especially when it comes to innovation. However, when the culture is right and people feel a part of the company's success, innovation thrives.

Remember the stories about Procter & Gamble and Hasbro? Both companies have enjoyed great success in the past several years, because they transformed their culture to enable innovation. When A. G. Lafley took over P&G, he had to get people into a collaborative mind-set and away from the hunkering-down mode they'd fallen into to protect their individual territories. He did this by creating an atmosphere that felt safer and more open to ideas than that of his predecessor. When Brian Goldner became CEO of Hasbro, he also got his people to engage at a whole new level. According to him, "What people needed to understand was that together they could do things that would never be accomplished by one person outside the team."

What both leaders were striving for, and in large part achieved, is the ideal culture for innovation. It's a culture where everyone from the top down knows his or her place in the innovation landscape and where people are empowered, nurtured, and rewarded. It's a culture where it doesn't matter if you're involved in category or operational innovation; you know your role is important and valued. It's a culture where innovation isn't a goal, it's a way of life.

In this chapter, we'll dissect the structure of the ideal innovation culture and look at "foundation attributes," the cultural must-haves that every company needs as the underpinning for successful innovation. Understanding what your organization can do to help innovation blossom will add another layer for you to build on when constructing your own innovation model.

To wrap up, we'll take a trip to the dark side. It's the antithesis of the ideal, a place where innovation killers like corporate politics, fear, control, and myopic vision muddle communication, confuse priorities, and derail progress. It's not a pretty picture. But it's one every leader needs to see, because sometimes, in order to build new worlds, you have to tear down old ones.

Growing an Innovation Culture

Over the past quarter century, both of us have worked with some of the most pedigreed companies in the world. We've also traveled the entire globe more than once and been exposed to nearly every cultural variation you can imagine. So when we set out to define the ideal culture for an innovation organization, we expected it to be a challenge. To our surprise, however, it was remarkably easy. While there might be thousands of unique characteristics for different cultural environments in the world, the characteristics of a healthy innovation culture were consistent. It didn't matter if the company was in the United States or Mexico, Italy or Russia, China or India or the Middle East; the key cultural characteristics remained the same. It also didn't matter if a company was involved in banking, petrochemicals, health care, technology, fashion, or soup; those companies that were truly innovative excelled at creating the same core cultural attributes.

Notice we said "excelled." Not only does a company have to have the right labels, which are often adopted when trying to evolve an innovation culture, it actually has to live the labels. Think of the culture as a garden and of innovation as the vegetables. You can have two identical gardens with the same soil, water, and sunlight. One looks great, filled with lush green plants, but the plants don't yield much produce. The other might not look as pretty, but the vegetables are prizewinners. The difference between the two is cultivation. Not only do you need to have the right ingredients, you have to prune, fertilize, and pick the vegetables off the plant as soon as they're ripe to allow more to grow. Too many times we say we value key attributes of innovation to make things look good, but the genuine substance is missing. People go by what they see and experience, not by what they hear. If you say it but don't do it, you may be showing off a great-looking garden, but you won't reap the full harvest that an innovation culture can provide.

As we talk about the core attributes for a healthy innovation culture, think about what is real, not what is said. Be honest. If you're a leader, ask yourself how you're demonstrating and developing each of these attributes in your own company, division, or group. Test your impressions by getting honest feedback from the people in your organization—and not just from your direct reports. It's best if you can elicit candid feedback in a nonthreatening environment where people don't fear reprisal. This may mean getting the feedback through an outside consultant who can guarantee respondents' anonymity or using a protected written method of feedback. If you have an executive team with a track record of telling you the truth even when it isn't what you want to hear, then using that team as a barometer can also be good.

If you're open to hearing the truth, whether it's positive or negative, then whatever is said will be helpful. You can only improve if you know and accept the reality of your situation. Once you know what you're dealing with, you can then take steps to ensure that these core elements are in place.

The Power of One: You Matter

In the most successful innovation cultures, everyone feels that they matter and bring something unique to the party. In companies where people feel they're just numbers, you get a lot less from them. Not only that, when people are undervalued, they flip into survival mode. If you don't take care of them, they have no choice but to take care of themselves.

Making people feel that they matter is something any good organization should do, not just for a select few, but for everyone who gets a paycheck with the company name on it. A culture that honors the individual provides a fair work environment based on merit and actual results, and it has a transparent evaluation system that provides clear measures of success. If this isn't the kind of environment you're used to, it may seem naive to expect to be treated so well, but it's not. Such cultures do exist in the real world. One of the best we've found is an Italian carmaker known not only for its high-performance machines but for the humanity of its culture as well. This is how the company describes what to expect when you work there:[2]

> Ferrari values the individual first. A person's freedom to express is given highest priority, because we believe this is the key to creative and successful team collaboration. The selection process (for employees) is detailed and precise— just what you might expect from a company that depends on meticulous and uncompromising attention to detail. Ferrari knows that the best performance is only achieved if employees feel empowered and appreciated. Ferrari also believes that the quality of its cars cannot be separated from the lives of the people working in their plants. That's why the working environment and welfare of the people working there are the most important priorities.

Because of this philosophy, the company is consistently voted as the one for which Italian university students would most like to work. Ferrari's employees regularly give the company high marks for employee satisfaction based on its commitment to the individual and his or her professional and personal development and well-being. Now ask yourself, does your company compare to Ferrari? If not, would you like it to? A rule of thumb we've lived by and observed in the best environments says that what you want for yourself is what you should provide for the people around you.

The Power of Team: Together We Can Do Anything

The strongest cultures of innovation demonstrate an amazing level of teamwork that maximizes people's strengths rather than focusing on their limitations. In fact, the focus is geared so strongly toward accomplishing great things and winning together that people feel compelled to help each other. This is reinforced in a million different ways, both spoken and unspoken.

A vibrant team culture has an abundance mentality that provides people with a sense of security that there's plenty for everyone. One person's success doesn't take a piece of the pie out of the equation for anyone else. This type of culture also assumes that you and your team not only *want* to do well, but that by working together, you *will* do well.

People know that their best chance of winning is to use everyone's strengths. When they see the power of teams in action, they long to be a part of those teams. This was a key factor in the success of many of the companies we've studied, but perhaps Sheri McCoy, worldwide chairman, Pharmaceuticals, and Executive Committee Member of Johnson & Johnson, said it best: "If you can get a team of people to focus their collective energy on the achievement of a goal that seems impossible without supporting each other, they will each rise above the potential they individually thought was possible. I have now personally experienced this truth in three completely different situations at Johnson & Johnson when I ran businesses in consumer, medical devices, and now in pharmaceuticals. Developing this esprit de corps doesn't happen overnight, but once it does, the business takes on whole new possibilities."

Innovation is definitely a team sport. And let's face it, teamwork is more fun and makes the odds of winning in the marketplace a whole lot higher. Developing a team-focused culture is a key part of the innovation environment's winning formula, and winning is always something people want to be a part of.

Solution Orientation: Empowerment Versus Fear

While it's important to work as a team, this doesn't mean people have to operate with one mind. Open interaction and healthy debate on the issues is critical in an innovation culture. The focus should be squarely on creating solutions, not on avoiding failures. More solutions will be found in an environment where helping each other find the solution to a problem is expected and rewarded. Jeff Bezos, CEO of Amazon.com, has an award that he gives to people who implement their ideas. The ideas don't even have to work, as long as they are well thought out. The key criterion is that the award only be given to people who execute their ideas *without* asking permission. Bezos has a cultural agenda that encourages people to take on solution-focused, innovative initiatives. He also recognizes that this happens more frequently if they don't have to jump through hoops to try new things.[3]

When a culture like this exists and empowerment conquers fear, profound changes can happen. We only have the time and energy we have. The question now is, how will we spend it? If people's emotional energy is used for fear and self-positioning, they'll have less to give to the organization. If, on the other hand, they spend virtually all their time and energy figuring out how the company can succeed, knowing that their leaders are strongly behind them, the results can be exceptional.

One way to cultivate this element of your culture is to frame how you approach challenges in positive language. Instead of focusing on a problem such as "What in the world happened here?," turn it around and ask, "How do we make this better?" When you phrase it this way, you will get imagination, discovery, and design instead of negation, criticism, and spiraling diagnosis.

You also have to have a process in place that enables true empowerment to flow through the company. For example, if someone on the front lines has a breakthrough idea inspired by customer interaction, how does this idea filter through the organization? If that person takes the idea to his or her boss and that boss doesn't see the merit, does it stop there? If so, are you really fostering empowerment? When people can present ideas and make decisions within a framework of acceptability, they feel more valued, creative, and energized. It is in this psychological space that the most imaginative ideas take hold and become innovation. An environment of empowerment is an environment of possibilities and new capabilities. Without empowerment, your organization will be limited in what it can produce by what you can personally identify or direct. With empowerment, your culture's ideas and creativity expand exponentially.

Trust, Honesty, and Transparency

While empowerment sets people free, our next core element ensures that they stay that way. People do their best work when they believe they're working with people they can trust. We tend to trust people when we know what they're doing and why. In organizations, this is called transparency.

There are a million ways we convey who we really are to those around us. People evaluate our honesty and trustworthiness both directly and indirectly based on the nonverbal cues we send. This is particularly true if you're a leader. Here are some questions to think about in the privacy of your own mind. Assume that your team has a positive track record, is smart and responsible, and exhibits a high degree of integrity.

1. Do you address issues candidly or dodge them by avoiding confrontation? If you dodge them, you risk adding another burden of responsibility to the strong performers who need your support and leadership.
2. Do you advocate honesty and transparency but then tell just part of the story, assuming your employees will never know the difference? If so, you may never know when they find out, but you will lose their respect.
3. When things take a legitimate downward turn, where are you? Do you do what you said you'd do, or do you disappear so people can't find you? Do you quickly retract funds you've committed? Do you immediately send an e-mail that distances you from the problem or blame someone else on your team? Well, guess what? Your people know exactly what you are doing, even

if they never call you on it. By dodging the bullet, you actually prove yourself untrustworthy as a leader. Stepping away from the issues tells your organization a lot about your integrity, courage and commitment (or lack thereof).

4. Do you say supportive things but model body language that makes you look angry or aloof? Be aware, if there is incongruity between words and unspoken communication, your people will go with the unspoken communication every time.

If your answer is yes to any of these, chances are you're communicating that you're not who you say you are. Once mistrust sets in, it fosters a sense of fear in your team and creates a culture of everyone for themselves. Worse still, the lack of transparency tells team members you don't think they're smart enough to catch on. Talk about disempowering and disenfranchising!

Innovation requires a lot of risk taking. Some of the risks are big, and some are small, but they are all risks, nonetheless. The best work gets done in an environment where what is said and what is done are the same, where you can count on the people above you and around you. Being honest with people provides the needed space for them to grow and do the right things for the business. It's the kind of environment where people are willing to take the right risks to excel and win in the marketplace.

A Celebration of Learning from Both Successes and Failures

In the world of innovation, the road is paved with a few big successes, a bunch of little successes, and lots of failures. That's why innovation is the elusive prize it is. What distinguishes a great innovation culture from the rest of the pack is that people celebrate learning from their failures as progress. When Thomas Edison failed at developing a working light bulb (for well over the nine hundredth time), he told his team they had just gotten a little closer to what would work by eliminating another variable they wouldn't need to try again.

Even today, General Electric celebrates failures that teach lessons that will lead to ultimate success. The company calls its corresponding award the Heroes of Failure Award. It goes without saying that we should reward successes, but why not also reward the brave soul who tries and fails, ultimately paving the road to success with lessons learned. When we celebrate learning from failure, we progress and grow, and growth is what it's all about.

Development and Training

Organizations like Procter & Gamble, GE, and Toyota are known for the great training they provide in key areas like marketing, finance, and general management. Providing your people with the tools and experiences they need to move their skills to the next level is critical, especially in an innovation-focused culture.

Also, since people spend two-thirds of their lives at work, the best companies don't stop at just professional training. Ferrari employees, in addition to continuing job education, also benefit from an extensive range of fitness and well-being programs. One, called Formula Benessere, raises health awareness and offers specialist checkups, while Formula Benessere Junior aims to foster an early interest in sports, fitness, and well-being in employees' children. Language lessons are also offered, along with an ongoing training program covering both the professional development and specific interests of employees. This helps create loyalty and gives the company's investment in talent a better return.[4]

Mentoring is also important, as it creates the opportunity for senior staff to link arms with the next generation. This provides continuity and an exchange of ideas between mature, seasoned players and rookies with bold, untried optimism and vision.

If you tie your leadership development initiatives directly to the strategic goals of your company, you will win on all counts. Company objectives will receive greater focus and attention, and your key people will get 80 percent of their developmental learning in areas that simultaneously drive growth and effectiveness (as well as innovation). With the right development and training, *everybody* benefits.

Clarity of Communication

We talked about the importance of communications in Part 2, but it bears repeating. In an innovation-focused environment, everyone should always understand what the company's vision is and what the strategy and key objectives are. Understanding these powerful directives is the glue that holds an organization together. In a successful innovation culture, everyone knows how what they're doing ties in to specific objectives. We've talked about seeing innovation as a tapestry with a multitude of colors woven together. When you have clear communication, your employees understand what the finished tapestry is supposed to look like. They know the color of their thread in the masterpiece that's being woven. They also know and appreciate what the other thread colors are and where those colors belong in the landscape. This specific understanding is what differentiates a great innovation culture from one that's simply good.

In the last chapter we introduced Durk Jager and A. G. Lafley, both CEOs at P&G, and how different their styles were. This was especially true of their communication methods. Where Jager was stern, Lafley was soothing. Where Jager intimidated, Lafley persuaded. He listened more than he talked. In short, he is living proof that the messenger is just as important as the message.

As CEO, Lafley didn't make grand pronouncements on the future of P&G. Instead, he spent an inordinate amount of time patiently communicating how he wanted the organization to change. In a company famed for requiring employees to describe every new course of action in a one-page memo, Lafley's preferred approach was the slogan. For example, he felt that P&G was letting technology rather than consumer needs dictate new products. So the new directive was "The consumer is boss." To make sure P&G worked closely enough with retailers, he dubbed the place where consumers first see the product on the shelf "the first moment of truth." "The second moment of truth" was the customer's experience at home.

Lafley used these phrases constantly, and they are still repeated throughout the organization today. At the end of a three-day leadership seminar he asked thirty young marketing managers from around the world what they'd learned. First on the list: "We are the voice of the consumer within P&G, and they are the heart of all we do." Lafley sat on a stool in front of the group and beamed. "I love the first one," he laughed, as the room broke into applause.

When he talks about his choice of words, Lafley is a little self-conscious. "It's *Sesame Street* language, I admit that," he says. "A lot of what we've done is to make things simple, because the difficulty is making sure everybody knows what the goal is and how to get there."

This is especially daunting in a global company where you have language and social differences that make clarity all the more important. But as challenging as diversity can be, it is also one of the richest sources of creativity.[5]

Embracing Diversity of All Kinds

The workplace today is a melting pot of cultures. In an increasingly globalized world, it's not unusual to have a host of people from different cultural backgrounds coming together to achieve a common organizational goal. That's a good thing. A diverse workplace fosters improved interpersonal communication and often ushers in a host of new ideas with roots in different cultures. Diversity builds employees' observation skills, as well as their skill at posing effective questions. A diverse workplace also translates into a better understanding of varied sections of society.

The real bonus in a diverse company, however, is diversity of thought. This is derived from experiences that team members bring to the table based on cultural heritage, age, geography, functional discipline, and business orientation. When you hire and cultivate diversity based on thinking styles, experiences, and perspectives, you're focusing as many lenses as possible on the company's objectives. The richer the input, the better the odds of creating innovation on all levels.

Becoming Customer Driven

Do you consider your customer to be your greatest asset or "the enemy" outside the gate? We spent a lot of time on this in Chapter 2 when we talked about insights. Your customers can be a continuing source of inspiration for every employee in the company—if everyone is open to them. It's easy to recognize that the individuals who are accountable for interfacing with customers are the people who need to be customer driven. In the most successful innovation companies, however, *everyone* believes they work for the customer. Whether you run a company or lead a division or functional group, your people should be clear that they don't work for you. They work for the customer, just like you do.

Jane and her family once took a VIP tour of Warner Bros. studios. From the parking lot attendant to the tour guide, ticket taker, and security guard, everyone was clearly focused on making the customer feel good. They said it was easy to do because the people running the company felt they were all working together to support the ultimate boss—the customer. Given that environment, it's not hard to imagine that good ideas for innovation are evaluated on their merit for customer satisfaction and not on personal agendas. The icing on the cake, however, was the fact that all of them, including the man serving gelatos at the end of the tour, when complimented on their performance, made it a point to say how much they loved working for "such a great company."

Networking and Connectivity

One of the most obvious yet underused tools for creating an innovation-focused environment is simply sharing ideas. This means connecting what you're doing with others both inside and outside the company. The more connected people are, the more they recognize how they can work together to make great things happen and the more great things *will* happen. This doesn't occur automatically, however. It starts at the very top. Ask yourself how much connectivity there is on the executive team. How well networked are top executives, both internally and externally? Is sharing applauded, or do politics promote isolation? These are important questions to understand when activating an innovation culture. The more your culture promotes interaction and collaboration with colleagues, competitors, and other businesses at large, the more innovative it tends to be.

Given the work Jane does, she sees a lot of top executives join new organizations. Those who jump right in and make things happen without building a strong network of understanding, connectivity, and support tend to start out strong but ultimately take much longer to create sustainable innovation and opportunity. Those who take the time to listen, understand, and appreciate the people around them may take longer to make new things happen, but once they do, they move quickly and in a way that allows people to feel ownership for the advances, thus encouraging more innovation.

Taking the time to listen and engage with those around you will never be a top priority in a crisis-driven, fear-based environment. These environments are too focused on the short term to see or reap the rewards that a networking-oriented, high-connectivity environment creates. Remember, you can never take advantage of opportunities to create new products, services, or markets if you don't know they exist. The cost of an insular environment will always be higher than you think. Why? Because you'll never know what you don't know.

Time to Think, Dream, and Create

In today's left-brain world, every minute is tightly assigned to an important task, even two or three important tasks at once. Technology enables us to be available and in motion every waking second, making us believe that we have to be "doing" all the time. Doing, however, is a reactive process. It's what's important when you know what needs to be done. Thinking and dreaming, though, is how you decide what needs to be done. Creating an environment where, at minimum, leaders make it a priority to think, dream, and create helps you know what the right things to do are. And this creates whole new opportunities for your business.

Before you panic and envision an environment with yoga mats in every office and a company mantra being hummed during the organization's daily hour of meditation and creation, be assured we're not suggesting that focus, deliverables, and accountability for deadlines are not important. Of course they are. What we are saying is that you will ultimately get more productivity and strategic upside from your organization if the environment has a whole-brain orientation that allows both the analytical and creative sides of the mind to flourish. This means there has to be time to reflect and imagine as well as to do.

The Estée Lauder Companies' president and CEO, Fabrizio Freda, schedules at least half an hour each day to just relax and imagine. He limits the amount of time he spends in meetings to forty-five minutes. He doesn't believe people who are stuck in a conference room are people who can innovate. An effective innovation culture requires clear focus, an understanding of what you're doing and why, and the space to think about the undefined white space that is around the bend just waiting to be developed and conquered.

If you give people the space to breathe mentally, you'll be pleasantly surprised to find that they actually get more done. Google has operated this way for years. The company not only wants but also requires its people to spend time exploring new horizons of interest. This keeps them fresh, learning, and expanding, and they've ended up generating the ideas for a number of Google's new business innovations, creating billions of dollars of market value. Netflix gives salaried employees unlimited vacation time. Operationally, this saves time and money for the company, which doesn't have to keep track of days used or pay out large sums of money for unused vacation time when someone leaves. Culturally, it conveys a sense of trust that engenders loyalty and allows people to control their own work-life balance.

Is your culture like those of Google, Netflix, or Ferrari, or does everything have to be done yesterday with little time to recover? When people are always on red alert, with constant high pressure, they move into what we refer to as "thrashing syndrome." In this condition, there's lots of activity and lots of drama, but there's no time to think. Thrashing will never achieve the best results for your business in either the short or the long term. Taking time to think, dream, relax, and create, however, will activate the innovation in your culture.

Ownership Empowerment

In an innovation culture, everyone in the organization feels empowered to make things happen. The ownership isn't driven on a top-down basis, with credit always flowing to the top. It is team focused. One of our favorite sayings is by Lao Tzu and creates the gold standard for leading an environment of ownership and empowerment: "A leader is best when people barely know he exists. When his work is done, his aim fulfilled, they will say, we did it ourselves." This is the ultimate in ownership empowerment—to not only see what is possible for the people in your organization to achieve, but also to create an environment that strengthens their belief in themselves to such an extent that they're actually more capable under your leadership than they would be on their own. Isn't this the level of impact we all want to have in the world? It's a worthy goal for everyone in general, but for an innovation culture, it's an imperative.

Micromanagement kills innovation, but empowerment allows it to flourish. Think about the most innovative, creative individuals you either know or have read about. Can you imagine Edison innovating in an environment where he was terrified to fail because his boss was looking over his shoulder every minute? Can you imagine Dean Kamen or Michelangelo creating their innovation masterpieces with a hierarchical figure breathing down their neck every second to ensure they achieved their goals? Always remember that the people you lead are not so different from you. Provide them with an environment where they can grow and thrive, and innovation will not be far behind.

Physical Space

So far we've been talking about cultural attributes that deal with the feeling and thinking side of innovation. Now we'd like to turn an eye toward the sensing side. Look around you. Does your operating environment encourage collaboration, or does it promote segregation? While having an open work environment that encourages collaboration doesn't guarantee that everyone will become innovators, it does reinforce the values you put in place regarding connectivity and networking. It also tends to open up the right-brainers in your midst. Remember, the space in which you work sends a strong message about the culture you value.

A number of years ago, Jane had an encounter with a Fortune 500 CEO while conducting a search for a head of facilities management for a consumer packaged-goods company that was planning to build a new headquarters . The meeting was to learn more about what the CEO wanted in the person who would be developing and driving the whole building project. Early in the meeting, Jane asked what she assumed would be an obvious question: "What do you want your new headquarters building to say to the world about the culture of the business?" The CEO stared blankly for a minute, then said he really hadn't thought about it, but maybe it would be a good point to consider.

That's exactly what A. G. Lafley thought about when he first took over as CEO at Procter & Gamble. The eleventh floor at P&G's corporate headquarters had been the stronghold of senior executives since the 1950s. Lafley did away with that thinking by moving all five division presidents to the same floors as their staff. Then he turned some of the vacated space into a leadership training center. On the rest of the floor, he knocked down walls so the remaining executives, including him, shared open offices. During his decade at the helm, Lafley sat next to the two people he talked to most frequently, which in true P&G style was officially established by a flow study: the head of human resources and his vice chairman, on whose marketing expertise Lafley relied.

He also made a significant change in the eleventh-floor conference room where he and his top executives met every week to review results, plan strategy, and set the agenda for the days ahead. When Lafley took over, the table was rectangular; he replaced it with a round one. People used to sit where they were told; with the round table, they sat where they wanted. If you walked into one of those meetings without knowing who was who, you'd have trouble picking out the top guy.[6]

Lafley was a master of this type of subtle communication, and the way he shaped the company's physical space said that everyone is important. This feeling of openness also makes it easier for people to interact with one another, and if they can make their space personal with photographs or mementos, it helps to promote creativity and ease as well. Eastern cultures have embraced this way of thinking about physical space for centuries. In recent years, the ancient principles of feng shui have also been adopted by many Western organizations to improve both the physical and energetic flow of their workplaces. Creative energy is at the heart of innovation. Anything you can do to increase positive energy while eliminating the negative kind is bound to pay off in innovation.

The Dark Side

When we began writing *Breaking Away*, we made a conscious decision to keep our focus on the positive as much as possible. There is value in negative examples just as there is value in failure, but we still believe that motivation and inspiration come from feeling good about yourself, your future, and the world around you. Having said that, we would be remiss in our mission to share our experience and expertise if we didn't spend a little time talking about the pitfalls into which so many companies stumble. We call it the Dark Side because, like a place void of light where little can flourish, it is a surefire innovation killer. Here are the four innovation assassins we find to be the most deadly when it comes to environment.

A Climate of Fear

The story goes that not too long after Joseph Stalin (a notoriously iron-fisted dictator) died, his successor, Nikita Khrushchev, was addressing the Supreme Soviet Council. As the new leader ranted about Stalin's terrible crimes, a voice called out, "Comrade, you were there. Why did you not stop him?"

Khrushchev stood glaring for a moment at the faces in the hall. Then he yelled, "Who said that? Show your face! I want to know who said that!" No one spoke. No hand went up. After a long and uncomfortable silence, Khrushchev said, "Now you know why."

Fear is a part of life, and unfortunately, it's often a part of work as well. People are afraid of making mistakes, looking stupid, crossing a controlling boss, or challenging cherished traditions and "the way we do things." When these fears exist, it not only limits employees' creativity and exhausts their energy, but it triggers their fight-or-flight instincts. When this happens, either you're constantly pushing against resistance to your ideas, as Durk Jager found at P&G, or you're losing your best people to the competition, sometimes in droves. No one likes to be constantly on the defensive. If your culture says mistakes, failures, or even just thinking too creatively are bad, then how can you expect anyone to take a chance?

As a leader of innovation, you can't eliminate fear in your organization, but you can reduce it by showing understanding, encouraging openness, being truthful, accepting intelligent failure, and welcoming the respectful challenging of ideas. If you currently have a culture that is steeped in fear, make it a top priority to change the climate. It will take time and commitment, but if you replace fear with a feeling of safety, the quality and speed of innovation will improve dramatically.

Politics as Usual

While so many leaders claim to believe that innovation is important and part of their charter, as Bill Ford says, people too often say yes and do no. That's because although everyone claims to be working busily on innovation, no one actually is. When this happens, the organization gets lost in a web of internal politics and positioning, and it loses focus on company objectives. Politics, whether internal or external, does little more than keep everyone's wheels spinning.

We've all heard about "winning the battle and losing the war." That saying can take on new meaning when you think about the energy that's spent on internal positioning such as beating the "competition" sitting at the next desk or one floor down. For most of us, this kind of environment is so common that we can't even imagine anything else. Remember when we talked about Bilal's experience at Kraft, where plant managers shared ideas and adopted a policy where the best were implemented even if it meant one of them might lose his or her job? Those managers were able to set politics and self-interest aside for the good of everyone. In the end, everyone was taken care of. Can you imagine something like that happening at your company? Most of us can't. The fact is politics, or fear of politics, is one of the biggest deterrents to innovation. Politics derails teamwork, encourages self-serving agendas, and undermines everyone's success.

The only way to take politics out of the mix is to change the reward system. If you make innovation the carrot instead of individual accomplishment, if you make "playing together for the good of all" the measure of success and recognition, politics will begin to fade. There will always be those whose self-interest will dominate their actions, but even they can be brought into the fold if getting ahead means taking up the innovation banner. It doesn't have to be politics as usual. What you're aiming for is one for all and all for one—the company.

Arrogance

We've all known people who were so convinced they knew everything that they closed themselves off to new ideas, wise counsel, and a helping hand when it was needed. This is the worst kind of leadership for innovation, because innovation at its core means being open and willing to accept the unknown. Arrogance keeps you insular and out of touch with your customers, your employees, and reality. It promotes a hierarchical culture that is internally and upwardly focused. When arrogance is coupled with a tyrannical leadership approach, as it often is, it ultimately encourages people to avoid risks at all costs. They become more focused on pleasing or hiding from the boss than on creating a company everyone is proud of. The sad thing about arrogance is that it often masks insecurities or a lack of self-esteem. If you're working for a leader who fits the know-it-all profile, there's probably not much you can do about it except take one for the team. If you have a great idea, make it his or her idea, and know that in the end this kind of character won't be around forever.

Myopia

While the innovation killers we've already talked about are pretty easy to spot, this one is more of a silent killer, something like heart disease. You often don't know you're suffering from it until it's too late. Myopia—or being shortsighted—can be seen in indiscriminate cost cutting to improve numbers, downsizing in the areas where innovation should flourish such as research or marketing, and keeping everyone so focused on next quarter that there's no time to think about the next decade.

Much of what we've talked about in this book so far is designed to combat myopia: exploring the four levels for opportunity, mining customers for insight, assessing risk, accepting responsibility, and building a great team and a great culture. But the first step in curing myopia is recognizing that it's there. It bears repeating that too often companies say they're committed to innovation but then don't follow through and ignite the engine. If you don't turn the key, you're not going anywhere, and the key is looking beyond today. There's a big future out there if you look at the horizon. And if you follow our final bit of advice in this chapter, you'll find it's easier than you think.

Keep It Simple

In all the companies we've worked in and researched for this book, one thing stood out as the foundation for an innovation-rich culture: simplicity. Make it easy for your people to understand what is expected. Be clear about objectives, and give employees the power to think and act in the best interest of the company. Don't encourage or accept hidden agendas. When there's only one agenda—a win-win for customers, employees, and the company—then no one can lose track of the mission.

Simplicity is about everyone knowing their place in the landscape and feeling like they're part of one community. It's about having the freedom to question and being given the respect of an answer. Simplicity is when rules are replaced with guidelines and self-promotion with self-esteem. When people have the same goal and understand what's expected of them, life is simple and they're happy to come to work. If they're happy, chances are you will be too.

You can't activate innovation alone. You need the company and all of its people behind you. When you understand the nuances of innovation, embrace responsibility through leadership, and activate the people around you, there's just one thing left to do and that's take it to market.

CHAPTER 9

Activating
the Market

Heads, You Win

You may have a barrelful of luck tomorrow.
If so, fine. But don't expect it, and most
of all, don't sit around waiting for it.

—HERMAN W. LAY

Throughout Mattel's history, innovation in toy design has led to historic products that have been passed from one generation to the next. Classics like See 'n' Say, Matchbox, and Hot Wheels (which has produced over a billion cars) are still popular after sixty years on store shelves. But of all the innovations the company is credited with, two clearly gave rise to its superstardom—and both were criticized as being too far-fetched to ever succeed. Ruth Handler, who cofounded Mattel with her husband, Elliot, and their business partner, Harold Matson, was responsible for both of them

A mother of two, Ruth was remarkably in tune with children. She paid attention to what they did, how they played, and what they watched on that new form of entertainment—the television. In the 1950s that meant "The Mickey Mouse Club." Every weekday for an hour, children across the country were glued to the small screen, as Mouseketeers sang and danced, wearing cheerleader-like costumes and giant mouse ears. For sixty minutes, kids were a captive audience—the same kids who played with the toys Mattel created. Even though toy marketing had traditionally been restricted to talking to parents through catalogs at Christmastime, Ruth kept wondering what would happen if she shook things up a little. What if, instead of toy manufacturers telling parents what their kids wanted, the kids told them? With a new product called a burp gun about to launch, and a no guts, no glory attitude, Ruth signed a one-year, $500,000 television advertising contract with Disney.[1] The commitment was nearly 10 percent of the company's sales revenue. People thought she was nuts. The commercials aired six times, and nothing happened. Then the Mattel people came back from a long weekend and couldn't open the door. The place was jammed with orders and reorders.[2] Ruth was vindicated.

Mattel's "Mickey Mouse Club" advertising, which plugged the Mattel name as hard as it did the burp gun, revolutionized the U.S. toy industry. The ad slogan "You can tell its Mattel— It's Swell!" was repeated by a generation of children, and it set the stage for Handler's second big coup.

About the same time Ruth was revolutionizing toy industry marketing, she was also working on another idea. Inspired by watching her daughter and her friends playing with paper dolls, she saw them dressing up the paper figures, projecting what the girls wanted to be when they grew up—and it wasn't just a mommy with babies. This piqued Handler's interest. While little girls had dolls to represent babies in a fantasy family, there were no three-dimensional grown-up dolls that could help them play out their own dreams. It was a void Ruth wanted to fill. A short while later, while on vacation in Germany, she saw Lilli, a full-size grown-up doll, and she knew she had her model. Despite the fact that Elliot said there was no market for such a toy, she pushed forward. For three years, she worked on perfecting the doll until she was finally ready to introduce it to the world.

The 11.5-inch-tall, buxom beauty, which was named Barbie after Ruth's daughter, made her debut at the 1959 American Toy Fair. Much to Handler's disappointment, it appeared her husband was right. "Half of our customers didn't want her," Elliot said.[3] Not willing to accept defeat, Ruth premiered the doll on TV. Even if the stores didn't want Barbie, she was convinced consumers would. After airing commercials on the "Mickey Mouse Club" in March 1959, with an ad jingle that said, "Someday I'll be just like you," Barbies flew off the shelves, along with all the specially made clothes and accessories. The consumers had spoken, and they said, "We love her!"

More than half a century later, it's reported that a Barbie is sold somewhere in the world every three seconds. Little girls and their mothers have bonded while playing with and collecting Barbies, even going on tweet-guided scavenger hunts with Mattel's latest innovation, Video Girl Barbie. None of this would have happened if Ruth Handler hadn't tuned into life around her and created both a remarkable toy and a way to take it to market with a message that clearly sold its appeal.

As we near the end of our exploration of innovation, it's time to take a bird's-eye view of one of the most important components of success—activating the market. You can have the best innovation imaginable, but if you can't convince the customer, you can't succeed. We'll start out by looking at some important rules of engagement, beginning with having a product that people actually want. This may seem self-evident, but you'd be surprised how many misses there are out there. The discussion will also include knowing where an innovation fits in the market, identifying its marketable value after customers have interacted with it in real life, and the importance of adapting and evolving as time goes on. As we go along, we'll talk about some of the avenues for customer engagement that are Marketplace Innovations themselves, such as social networking, global sales forces, friends, and tweets. It's an ever-changing world, and staying hooked into it is not only how innovation is inspired, it's how it's delivered too—at least when you do it right.

Heads You Win, Tails You Lose

One of the biggest disappointments a company can experience is when it has gambled enormous amounts of time, money, and resources on developing an innovation only to have it fail in the marketplace. In fact, more than 70 percent of new offerings flop in the first year. Included in that number are innovations that should work but don't. Sometimes the reasons are obvious—the company didn't do its homework on the customer, the timing is wrong, or the adoption rate is too slow for needed return. These are problems that can be avoided by aligning the three Ws we talked about in Chapter 4. But even if you do have alignment—that is, a product customers say they want, the technology to pull it off, and a clear way for it to make money—in today's volatile climate, it can still feel like everything is riding on the flip of a coin. You can, however, rig the outcome in your favor by thinking ahead.

Before you take an innovation to market, make sure your cross-functional launch team (marketing, sales, R&D, and finance) has worked through these five crucial elements of engagement: purpose, fit/positioning, real value, clear communications, a way to build momentum. As always, make sure you have the ability to adapt and evolve through continuous customer feedback. By making sure all of these elements are covered, you'll have a much better chance of being in that 30 percent that wins the coin toss.

What Were You Thinking?

It's amazing how many innovations are launched because companies think customers want one thing, when in reality they don't, or at least not in the way it's been created. This is one of the greatest pitfalls in innovation—thinking you know what customers want just to have them surprise you. But the truth is a product can't be called a hit until the customer calls it one. No one knows this better than R.J. Reynolds. In 1988, the company, responding to increasingly negative press about secondhand smoke, came up with a "smokeless" cigarette. Smokers seemed to like the idea. It would relieve some of the pressure from non-smokers and eliminate some of the distasteful consequences of smoking, like the ashy smell in clothes and hair and the sootlike residue left in the environment. The idea was so promising, in fact, that the company spent $325 million to develop it. There was only one small problem. As *Reporter Magazine* so elegantly put it, "It produced a smell and flavor that left consumers, and those around them, retching." The cigarettes, called Premier, lasted four months on the market. Not one to give up, in 1996 the company spent another $125 million on an updated version called Eclipse. It fared no better.[4]

What R.J. Reynolds failed to take into account is the fact that smoking is a sensory experience. While you don't have people going around saying their cigarettes taste good, they also don't think they taste bad. So while customer research might have indicated a desire for a smokeless cigarette, the respondents didn't want it at the expense of the experience. The trade-off wasn't worth it. That's a huge consideration in innovation. You have to know what people are giving up. If it's comfort with the familiar, you can have a problem. When early ecofriendly products came out, people liked the idea of helping the environment, but if a detergent or hand soap didn't lather, it was too far afield from what they were used to. When they didn't see lather, they didn't think "clean." Add to that the increased cost, and widespread adoption was difficult to achieve.

How people feel about an innovation also depends on how it makes them feel about themselves. This is a critical part of market engagement. Self-esteem and feeling important and respected are values to which everyone responds. If your innovation enhances these values, flaunt them! If your offering diminishes them, you're probably in trouble. And yes, it is actually possible for an innovation to make people feel bad about themselves.

It's no secret that single adults aren't always into cooking for themselves, but they still have to eat. Since simplicity and convenience are two things to which people respond well, Gerber, the baby-food manufacturer, came up with what it thought was a brilliant Marketplace Innovation: adult foods in a jar. Easy to buy, store, and use, it seemed a surefire way to expand the company into a whole new arena. Unfortunately, the execution left a lot to be desired. It seems the target audience—college students and single adults—had no interest in eating creamed beef out of a baby-food jar. The name of the product, Singles, couldn't have helped either. According to Susan Casey in the October 2000 issue of *Business 2.0*, "They might as well have called it *I Live Alone and Eat My Meals from a Jar.*"[5] The product was a complete disaster.

If you think about it from the consumer's perspective, it's no wonder. Although Gerber Singles made sense from the company's point of view (after all, it could save manufacturing costs by using the same jars it used for its baby food), no consumer was interested in buying a product that not only told the world that he or she was alone, but also thrust them back to infancy—

something newly independent college students clearly wouldn't respond to.

So even though both R.J. Reynolds and Gerber were clearly innovative, the first with a technological advance that could have changed the entire industry and the second with a Marketplace Innovation that could have garnered the company a huge new audience, they lost millions of dollars because they weren't ready with products that people wanted—at least not the way they were.

Looking for the Perfect Fit

Clearly a primary purpose of innovation is to expand into new markets to create sustainable growth. Part of that involves coming up with new products that don't cannibalize existing lines. But sometimes, like with Gerber, a plausible idea is only good if there's a fit with the intended consumer. Instead of targeting college students, Gerber may have had better luck marketing its strained foods to the elderly either directly or through extended-care facilities. In this way, the company would have tapped into the two times in a person's life cycle when soft, healthy food fit consumer needs. When you're bringing an innovation to market, positioning—or in the case of our next example, repositioning—can uncover huge opportunities and avenues for further line innovations.

Oil of Olay, created by Graham Wulff, an ex-Unilever chemist, originated in South Africa in 1949. Packaged in a heavy glass bottle, the pale pink, silky fluid with a delicate scent was a radical departure from the heavy beauty creams of its time. It looked good, felt good, and smelled good. The women who tried it loved it.

As different as the product was, however, the way it was marketed was even more unusual. Targeted to the over-twenty-five crowd, neither the package nor the advertising mentioned what the product actually did. The only clue appeared in ads that used copy such as "Share the secret of a younger-looking you" and talked about the "beauty secret" of Oil of Olay. It created an air of mystery and allure that women couldn't help but respond to.

Wulff and his marketing partner, Jack Lowe, also went about distribution in an unorthodox way. Instead of going to retailers to place the product, they waited for pharmacies to ask for it, based on customer demand pushed by advertising. The strategy and the product both performed beyond expectations. For three decades, the pink beauty fluid spread across the globe.

When Procter & Gamble acquired Oil of Olay in 1985, the brand had stabilized at annual sales of $200 million. With the power of P&G behind it, however, the company had even bigger plans for the pink stuff in the bottle. One of the objectives of P&G at that time was to increase its presence in the beauty/skin care space. To that end, Susan Arnold, then president of global personal beauty and global feminine care, was given full reign to create magic. The first thing she did with Olay was drop the word *oil*, which suggested a heavy or greasy texture no longer valued in skin care products. Then she embarked on a full-blown brand makeover. "It used to be known as the mysterious pink beauty fluid and your grandmother's brand," said Arnold. "We relaunched Olay with the tagline 'love the skin you're in' speaking to both inner and outer beauty and began going after the higher end of the market with anti-aging products."[6] This strategy was definitely a gamble, considering the channels through which the product was sold.

The customers of the pharmacy chains and bargain-priced retailers were used to shopping on price, but Arnold was convinced that if she delivered the product and conveyed its value, consumers would come around. It took some campaigning to get her retail customers to go along, but she convinced them that as long as the cost was still less than department and specialty store brands women would want this affordable indulgence. She was right. She found her perfect fit, and from there, a clear path for growth emerged.

New items that were spurred off of the first line of "beauty fluid" included Olay Daily Facials cleansing cloths, an upgrade of Olay's Total Effects line, and an upgraded formulation to the original moisturizer line. The brand also debuted Regenerist, a moisturizer to help renew the appearance of skin. This broadening of the line not only made money, it expanded its audience from serving mostly baby boomers to encompassing Gen Xers and even the younger Generation Y as well.

With momentum building, the company accelerated the pace of innovation by partnering with small biotech companies, universities, and major suppliers. According to Arnold, the Olay brand alone had more than fifty external collaborations in progress. The brand that started out at $200 million hit the billion-dollar mark in 2003 and, in 2009, was responsible for $2.8 billion in revenue.[7] Right from the beginning, this product knew where it belonged in the marketplace. Under the stewardship of the master innovators at P&G, it has provided enormous growth for the company, with the promise of more to come. Knowing your customers and consumers so well that you can, as in this case, literally get under their skin keeps you market nimble and engaged in a way that not only will ensure success, but will keep the innovation pipeline flowing for years to come.

Seeing the Trees in the Forest

While knowing your customer and where you fit in the marketplace are critical first steps, they are just first steps. As your offering makes its way through the customer experience, new insights will come to light. This is where market agility becomes as important as the innovation itself. In fact, sometimes you can actually have the better offering and still end up outside the winner's circle, because you didn't adapt to new information as the customer gained experience with the product. This is especially true when your innovation is at the transformational or category level. At these levels, people can't possibly know what they want until they experience the innovation for a while in real life. If your competition is more astute at picking up on these nuances, then better product or not, you're in trouble.

A classic case of competition outmaneuvering the forerunner of an innovation happened during the battle for the home video market in the 1970s.[8, 9] Sony first introduced the home video recorder in 1975. Built on its Betamax format, the machine was a completely unique innovation in home entertainment that captured the imagination of consumers. Best of all, the company was alone in the field. It would be at least a year before competitor JVC released another video recorder, the VHS, built on its own proprietary format. The appearance of a rival on the scene wasn't unexpected, but Sony didn't realize that while it might have won the battle to get to market first, it was about to lose the war.

First of all, in its rush to be the groundbreaking technology, Sony appears to have misjudged the potential of the home video market. Because it was the first out and had a comfortable window as the sole provider, Sony was sure it could establish Betamax as the leading format. It was so confident, in fact, that it took its time nailing down other manufacturers to license the technology. JVC's parent company, on the other hand, quickly licensed its VHS format. While Sony agreements were languishing in a to-do pile, JVC's deals were cut, and Beta's fate was sealed.

By early 1977, every major consumer electronics company of the era had its own brand of a VHS-formatted VCR at a significantly lower retail price than Sony's Betamax. Since the two formats, Beta and VHS, were incompatible, that meant consumers had to choose between the two. It was a no-brainer. There were more brand choices in the VHS format and lower prices because of the competition, so VHS usually won out. That was misstep number one. Unfortunately, it didn't end there.

Don't Just Listen—Hear

When an innovation is introduced to the market, there's naturally a learning curve for both the customer and the company. Testing only gives us limited insight of use and preferences. This insight is often influenced by the company through its testing methods. Too often, what we hear is what we hope to hear. It's sort of like asking people if they want black or white instead of asking what color they prefer. In the case of VCRs, Sony believed that picture quality was what customers valued above all else. Unfortunately, customers didn't agree.

To deliver the quality it wanted, Sony had to stick to a one-hour format for both recording and playback. This format, however, didn't allow enough time to record an evening of primetime programming or, more importantly, Monday night football. Quality was nice, but what people really wanted was time. They wanted their football games and an afternoon of soap operas and Hollywood movies in their living room, all of which required time. The consumer spoke, but Sony wasn't listening. JVC, however, was all ears. It almost immediately began modifying its machines to tape for longer periods, providing a "perfect for movies," built-in, two-hour playback time.

Being able to watch feature-length films at home was a major breakthrough. It not only transformed consumer habits, it ensured wide adoption and longevity of the VHS format. In the end, it was this movie-playback capability that both spawned the huge video rental business that flourished in the 1970s and 1980s and firmly established VHS as king.

The amazing thing about this story is that, overall, Sony *did* have the better product. Consumers even believed that Sony's Betamax was superior and said in testing that all things being equal, they preferred to purchase a Betamax. When push came to shove, however, they didn't make the leap. They wanted an *affordable* VCR, and they wanted *time*, both of which JVC provided.

In 1988, Sony succumbed and began to market its own VHS machines. Despite claims that the company was still backing Beta, it was clear that Beta was dead. Today, the only remaining aspect of the Betamax system is the slang term *betamaxed*, used to describe something that had a brief shelf life and was quickly replaced by the competition. JVC, on the other hand, dominated the home market for thirty years and collected billions in royalty payments.

In the end, the deciding factor wasn't the innovation at all; it was large-scale market activation. Both companies developed breakthroughs with the potential to transform the home entertainment market. Both had powerful, well-established brands. The balance began to tip when JVC licensed its technology, activating the trade segment and strengthening its business case. JVC got to the sweet spot when new consumer insights surfaced and it made adjustments that activated the consumer segment. You can't just be good, you have to be in tune. And it doesn't hurt to have a way with words.

Trust Me, It's Good For You

Engaging the market is as much about communications as anything else. Not only do you have to have something that people want, they have to understand—at least on some level—why they want it. If they don't, it ends up being something like a parent telling a child to eat vegetables "because I said so." It doesn't work with kids, and it doesn't work with customers. Since innovations are by definition unique, people often need to be educated about the value of the offering in order to embrace it.

We have talked about Apple often in this book because, let's face it, the company is really good at what it does, especially with marketing. The iMac was a great little machine, but its introduction to market was pure genius. If you'll recall, the biggest barrier to adoption of the Internet in homes was how difficult it was for the average person to get online. With C drives and HTML language, as well as the whirring, beeping, and gurgling followed by unexplained pauses you got with most computers, it just didn't work for the faint of heart—until iMac and a commercial that said it all.

"Presenting three easy steps to the Internet," a voice announced. "Step one, plug in. Step two, get connected." As the screen faded to a rotating view of the brightly colored, completely unintimidating iMac, the voice continued, "Step three. [quiet laughter] There is no step three. There's no step three!"

This from a company that, until those commercials, the average person didn't even know existed. Genius at communicating value and branding both the company and its products, all it takes now is a whisper that Apple is coming out with a new product and orders start pouring in. In 2010, when it introduced the iPad, it sold 3 million units in the first eighty days.[10]

Everything Apple does, from the creative, direct simplicity of its advertising to its sleek, sexy packaging and accessible instructions and tutorials, communicates value. The only disaster we've seen from the company in this area was the ahead-of-its-time Newton. The ads were full of mystery and innuendo, but it never really engaged the market. You were left with this burning question: what the heck does it do?

Since the idea of a personal digital assistant was new, people couldn't make the connection. The advertising never said how it could impact their lives. Creating buzz is one thing, but buzz only goes so far. Innovation is about making life better, happier, simpler, more fun, or more meaningful. Don't leave it up to consumers or customers to figure it out on their own.

BioPlastics, an Ohio-based manufacturer of plastic-coated webbing material, innovated a product for ambulance and hospital gurney straps. Traditionally these straps, used to secure patients who are being transported, are made of porous nylon that absorbs fluids and unsavory microbes. By law, the straps have to be replaced after every use. The new product was completely coated with a soft, flexible plastic that could easily be washed and disinfected. This not only extended the use of the product, it cut down on cleanup time and made it much safer for patients and crew. With so much going for it, it had just two barriers to adoption: price and a limited marketing budget. BioPlastics needed to communicate the value of the product quickly with each exposure. It found the solution in the product name, calling it BioSafe. The manufacturer then launched a two-tiered, targeted campaign that spoke to crews about safety and ease and to chief financial officers about cost-effectiveness and reduced liability for employee and patient exposure to pathogens. The company is now on its third generation of the product. It has expanded into adjacent industries like biomedicine, sports, and recreation. It has even had some of its products in outer space.

What Apple, BioPlastics, and the earlier story about Mattel all show us is how important it is to identify what makes an innovation unique, valuable, and worthy of exchange and to communicate all three clearly and effectively. To drive home the importance of being clear in your communications, consider this: According to the Newspaper Association of America, a decade ago, the average American was exposed to more than three thousand advertising messages in the average day. With the addition of all the electronic media today, you can probably get that many before breakfast! Everyone is trying to build a brand, so it's especially important, when you're launching something new, to get through the clutter. Know what you have and communicate it clearly. If you do, then the best engagement tool of all will take place—evangelism.

Fanatic Fans— Building Momentum

If you have the right product, it's positioned properly in the market, and you've built a communications platform that clearly articulates the unique value of your innovation, what you need now is a base of fans who will serve not only as your early adopters but as your evangelists as well. Where you'll find them depends a great deal on what type of innovation you're dealing with. If it's a Transformational or Category Innovation, your early adopters will likely be on the fringes—the die-hards in your industry, whether that is electronics, science, sports, day trading, or purchasing. You can learn a lot from them, and you need to. Because these two types of innovation involve mostly untried ventures, education is likely to be a significant part of building your audience. That being the case, you need to understand what is intuitive about your innovation and what needs explanation.

For example, when ATMs first came out, it was necessary to have very precise instructions for use, because how they worked really didn't relate to common experiences in people's lives. You'd see people standing in line with puzzled looks on their faces, reading every word. Then there would be this look of amazement when money appeared. Now it's so routine that people whiz through the process. Little kids actually think that's where money comes from! Once people were familiar with ATM use, debit cards for shopping became an intuitive leap that wasn't hard to make. This is where knowing the adoption rate of similar innovations helps plan your market engagement strategy, especially in Transformational or Category Innovation. The same can be true of Marketplace and Operational Innovation, but quite often there is at least some familiarity with innovations on these levels, so momentum is easier to gather.

Take Spanx, for example. We talked about Sara Blakely's body-shaping innovations in Chapter 2. While in innovation terms, adoption of her products was relatively fast (she went from a $5,000 start-up in 2000 to a $150 million business within seven years), it might not have been so without a little help from her friends. Tireless and shameless in her efforts to get her products some attention, Sara called friends and asked them to go to stores and buy them out so they'd have to order more. She also recruited her Tri Delta sorority sisters and sent out countless samples, calling on producers and editors and asking them to "discover" her product. Over the next year, Spanx was featured on "The Oprah Winfrey Show," "The Today Show," "The View," "The Tyra Banks Show," CNN, and countless other television programs and news channels, as well as in the pages of *Forbes*, *Fortune*, *People*, *Entrepreneur*, *In Style*, the *New York Times*, *USA Today*, *Glamour*, and *Vogue*. Before long, Spanx had a following. The following became a fan base, and the fan base became a loyal market.

As a new company with a new product, Spanx had to start from ground zero to build its fan base. If you're an established brand, you have a much easier job of it. Especially if you come up with a way to keep people connected to you through more than product purchases. This "more" can be education, such as the American Express Small Business Idea Hub that features discussions and expert advice for entrepreneurs. As a continuing source of information, the company has a natural platform to introduce new offerings.

The Estée Lauder brand has this marvelous "let's play make-over" feature on its website that allows a woman to upload her own photograph and virtually try new makeup looks. Using the individual makeup elements like foundation, blush, eye shadow, and lipstick, customers can mix and match their own color combinations or click on a particular Estée Lauder "look" to see how it's put together and how it will look on them. Their faces change miraculously, right on the screen. It's not only fun, it helps take some of the guesswork out of buying makeup. What's more, it gives the company a platform from which to launch new products to its most loyal customer base. As your fan base grows, it greatly decreases adoption time and improves return on investment.

The key here is evangelism. Think of it this way: If you tell two people, and they each tell two people, and then every day each person tells two more, in a few weeks that initial contact has grown from two to more than half a million. In our digital and socially networked world, that's not so far-fetched. Today, every company from Abbott Laboratory to Xerox has a Facebook page with thousands of "friends" signed up. Twitter is almost mandatory in some arenas like publishing, entertainment, and sports. We even know of a dentist who has his office tweet patients if he's running behind so they can adjust their schedules if they want to. He's also the one who's progressive enough to show movies in the treatment rooms, so it's not a surprise that he's embraced this form of communication. The point is there are so many ways to connect with the consumer that there's almost no excuse not to make evangelism an integral part of market engagement.

One company that wanted to launch a subscription-based marketing newsletter started off with a free version that it encouraged recipients to forward to colleagues. It did this by simply putting "please forward" in the subject line. The product was so good that people did forward it, often recommending that friends and colleagues subscribe. This same strategy would work with a white paper, educational articles, and even success stories if they contain worthwhile material. If it's free and it's good, people will share it. That is evangelism at its best. If you build evangelism, you build momentum. Once that happens, innovation adoption is suddenly much easier.

One final word on evangelism before we move on. It's so easy to focus on technology when we talk about reaching the market, because we're a hyperconnected world. But as a wise friend once observed, for all our "connection," we seem more alone than ever. Evangelism, at its very heart, is about people loving something so much they want to share it. And that doesn't just apply to customers; it should also apply to your sales force and your channels.

When an innovation is being launched, everyone in the company should celebrate it, talk about it, and get their excitement behind it—even if it's not their product or in their business unit. If sampling is part of your launch strategy, don't stop at consumers; include the channel, employees, and strategic partners.

If you have forty thousand people in your company, and each person told just two people about this great new product or service the company was introducing, imagine the impact. Even if it isn't something everyone uses, you never know where the seed will land. A colleague told us about sitting next to someone on a plane who mentioned a new inventory tracking system his company had just released. She mentioned the conversation to her brother, who ended up being one of the technology's early adopters. He never would have known about it if it hadn't been for that chance encounter.

Engaging the market is about bringing all the forces—human and otherwise—together to introduce something unique to the world. You don't want it to be a small sputter, you want it to build and build and then burst through the gates with all the excitement of the running of the bulls at Pamplona! Innovation isn't just some new flavor of the month. If it's unique, valuable, and worthy of exchange, it's worth getting excited about, and if you're excited, others will be too.

Closing the Loop

If you look at market engagement as an eternal loop, then the driver that keeps it spinning is this last element—continuous customer feedback. Customers not only give us inspiration for innovation, they let us know when we're on track, when we're not, and when we need to tweak something to make good even better. We've seen this time and again with the companies we've talked about, but perhaps nobody knows this better than Amazon.com. In fact, the company built its business on it.

In less than a decade, Jeff Bezos turned a business he operated out of his garage into one of the most recognizable brands on earth. Amazon.com came of age with the Internet, and even though its customers never see or talk to a live person, it is still renowned for its customer experience and overall satisfaction.

Once the world's largest bookstore, as a result of Category and Operational Innovations, it now offers the world's largest selection of just about everything. Whether you want to buy new kitchenware or baby clothes; browse every conceivable title of new and used CDs, DVDs, and books; or contribute a few dollars to your favorite presidential candidate, an online universe of commerce is a mouse-click away. Visit the site once, and when you return, Amazon.com remembers your name, the items you bought the last time you visited, and the items you browsed—all so that it can recommend other titles or products that might interest you the next time you shop.

To maintain this level of customer interaction and experience takes constant assessment of what customers like and dislike supported by constant innovation. Using its own proprietary software and the software of business intelligence giant SAS, Amazon continually uses a test-and-learn approach for evaluating every new product, page layouts, and search technology, giving it a significant edge in the "adapt and evolve" game.

"We do a lot of work that's focused on understanding whether ideas that different groups have developed actually have a positive impact on the customer experience," explains Diane N. Lye, Ph.D., Amazon's senior manager for worldwide data mining. "With SAS, we analyze all the data to determine whether different design enhancements improve the quality of the page and ultimately the overall customer experience. On a typical experiment, we might have seventy metrics." This gives the company the ability to measure the impact of any innovation as soon as it's launched. "When we roll something out," she adds, "we simultaneously know what it's going to do for the business and for the customer."[11] With that kind of continuous feedback, the company can make decisions that push adoption of successful innovation while limiting risk if something unexpected comes up.

While not everyone has Amazon's capability to assess innovation on the fly, it's important to devise a means to find out what customers are thinking and then allow them to be a part of the innovation journey. Earlier we wrote about Ford and how it recruited a hundred people to try out the Fiesta and record their feedback on Facebook. That not only helped build momentum, it provided Ford with a valuable feedback stream. AAA auto club, as part of its innovative On the Go roadside assistance program, has an on-the-spot battery replacement service. Post-service, an auto club representative calls to see how everything went, getting instant feedback.

Setting up a feedback system when you go to market is as important as orchestrating its debut. With today's technology, it's easier to do than ever. In fact, uncensored opinions on almost any product, service, or company are usually just a tweet away. Ask and you'll surely receive—probably more than you want. But like the flood of input you receive that can inspire the beginnings of innovation, this feedback is what you need to close the loop and keep the flow of energy moving. When you do, you help innovation reach its full potential and also allow it to spiral into new avenues of growth. All you have to do is grab hold and let feedback take you, your company, and your customers to greater heights.

Avoiding the Pitfalls of Activation

All that we've talked about so far—having the right product, listening to customers and consumers, communicating value, building evangelism, and engaging in continuous customer feedback—are essential steps to winning in the marketplace. We know this. Yet too often we fall short because we get stuck in outdated methods and thinking that is more product-centric than customer focused. This never works with innovation. To close this chapter, we have one more story. It's about a company that lost and then found its way, saving an excellent innovation from certain demise. There are lessons for all of us in its journey and more than a little hope.

When Eastman Chemical Company developed a breakthrough clear, rigid packaging material, it knew it had something special. With it, the company could make large containers that were food grade, had excellent clarity, and had the design flexibility to be molded with an integrated clear handle. The product was launched in 2003, supported by traditional segmentation, targeting, and promotional techniques. Interest was high, but unfortunately, revenues weren't. Ultimately, research showed that while customers liked the innovation, they didn't like it enough to pay for it.

Faced with failure, Eastman took a step back and recognized three things: (1) its culture was steeped in a manufacturing heritage that put up more barriers than support for innovation activation; (2) marketing had little input in strategic growth initiatives, so all the team saw was product, not customer; and (3) Eastman had little customer insight on which to base its launch decisions. In short, it needed to figure out not only where to play in the market, but how to execute its plan. To do that, it had to get out of its own way. With the help of Monitor Group, a global management consulting firm, that's what it did.[12]

In the past, Eastman had identified market opportunities by keying in on product attributes like molding and materials processes and functional benefits like clarity, flexibility, and price. In other words, the features/benefits game. Segmentation efforts were even more loosely defined as simply being large, medium, or small targets. The new strategy, however, had the organization focusing on direct-packaging customers as well as on other downstream members of the supply chain. This included brand owners, retailers, and consumers.

Opening up the vista in this way allowed Eastman to see who would most value an innovation's attributes, like design flexibility, and be willing to pay for it. What the company found was that the segment it had always thought of as its most logical—packaging manufacturers—was interested in only one rather small benefit of the innovation. To these customers, it wasn't worth the extra cost. How many times do we do this—stay within our comfort zone, and when we fail there, assume it's the innovation's fault?

Fortunately, with Monitor's help, Eastman avoided that pitfall and found brand owners. Constantly battling for consumer attention, beverage companies were looking for a container that stood out from the ordinary bottles that crowded store shelves. Even better, they were willing to pay for it.

Armed with this insight, Eastman developed an activation plan to tell the right story to the brand owners. In an even greater departure from its ordinary approach, it also developed tools to help prospective customers sell the innovation to their internal stakeholders. For the first time, Eastman's sales force could extend its reach beyond its contacts into the inner sanctums of prospect companies. The strategy paid off. In 2006, POM Wonderful, an innovative producer and marketer of pomegranate juice, became Eastman's first customer. When POM introduced its new, clear-handled container in its iconic figure-eight-shaped bottle, juice sales took off. *Newsweek* described POM as the company that "single-handedly transformed the ungainly pomegranate into a stylish libation."

When POM caught the attention of consumers, it wasn't long before competitors took notice too. The next to sign up was a global beverage company. Eastman now officially had an innovation that met all the criteria: it was unique, it was valuable, and to brand owners and consumers alike, it was definitely worthy of exchange. It wouldn't have happened if the company hadn't recognized the need to internally activate its people and to make the changes necessary to identify and engage the right market for its innovation.

You don't always have to get it right the first time, but if you have the courage to try again—to align your innovation with your customer and your business needs—you can turn what looks like a failure into a roaring success.

CHAPTER 10

Activating You

Ready, Set, Go

Do not attempt to walk through life without a dream,
without a hope, without a goal to achieve success.

—LUIS NOBOA NARANJO

n May 2002, Satoru Iwata became Nintendo's fourth president since the company was founded by Fusajiro Yamauchi in 1889. Only forty-three years old, the new president had been preparing for this job most of his life. He created his first games during high school. While still in college, he took a job selling computers just to spend the day playing with them. After graduation from the Tokyo Institute of Technology, Iwata and some fellow geeks formed a software development company called HAL Laboratory, Inc. "My father didn't talk to me for about six months after I joined HAL," he says.[1] Fortunately, that didn't stop him.

Despite his parent's concerns, it was clear from the beginning that Iwata was talented. A passionate and astute programmer, he used elegant yet simple code that earned him cult status among programmers. This wasn't his only gift though. He also had a keen sense of the video game industry and maybe a little luck on his side. Nintendo, HAL's primary client, had just released the Family Computer (known as the Nintendo Entertainment System in America), and the gaming world was about to change. Over the next several years, Iwata and his team developed a string of classic games for Nintendo. Even so, all wasn't well with HAL. In 1992, the company was on the verge of going under until Iwata took over as president. His ability to make decisive moves to save the company not only revived HAL, but it also caught the interest of Hiroshi Yamauchi, president of Nintendo. As it turned out, Iwata was being closely watched, and his success with HAL ultimately led him down a path for which he seemed destined. When he joined Nintendo in 2000 as chief of the corporate planning division, he not only had a track record, he had a plan.

As the sophistication of technology evolved, games were becoming increasingly complex. That meant they were more expensive to develop, and as a result, profitability for the entire industry was dropping. Iwata recognized this as a negative trend and felt it really wasn't what customers wanted. Most games were story based and hard to play; the difficulty kept casual players away. For those who did play, once the story was cracked, the game lost its allure. Iwata's goal was to make new games simpler, fun to play, and fun to repeat even for beginners. What's more, by giving customers what they wanted, company profits would increase because of shorter, less expensive development time. It was back to basics, and it worked.

Nintendo generated a staggering 41 percent increase in profits to $953 million on sales of $4.4 billion at the end of fiscal year 2001 and boasted a 20 percent increase in sales over the previous year.[2] This made naming Hiroshi Yamauchi's successor in 2002 pretty easy.

Since then, under Iwata's leadership, Nintendo has brought hundreds of thousands of new people into gaming. His "keep it simple, keep it fun" approach to innovation led to the development of one of the most successful products in video game history—the Wii. It took five years from concept to introduction to bring the innovation about, but when it hit, it hit big. People loved the simplicity, the experience, and the system's inclusive nature (anyone from a four-year-old to an eighty-year-old could learn to use it with relative ease). The graphics were flat and unsophisticated, but no one seemed to mind. The Wii brought motion to video games, turning televisions into everything from bowling alleys and tennis courts to boxing rings and undersea classrooms complete with hidden treasure. Best of all, the whole family could play together. It was perfect! It left everyone else in the dust.

When Wii launched in September 2006, it sold more than 3 million units by the end of the year. In fact, it was so popular that many stores sold out as soon as new shipments arrived. By the end of 2007, net profits had increased by more than 500 percent. Through mid-2010, more than 73 million Wiis could be found in homes around the world, making it the number-one console in the industry.[3]

But success sometimes creates its own problems, and Nintendo has had its share. In the 2009 financial year, the company experienced its first drop in net profits in six years to "just" $2.4 billion.[4] The explosive growth has stretched the company's resources, and time to innovate has been hard to come by. Much to Iwata's credit, however, the problems haven't been ignored. Partnering with outside companies to relieve some of the pressure, he has once again turned Nintendo's focus to innovation. With new offerings in the wings, there's no doubt the company has more surprises in store.

Passion, focus, and an intuitive connection to the marketplace are hallmarks of Iwata's tenure so far. His success didn't come by throwing millions of dollars at the wall and hoping something would stick. It happened by getting back to basics, building the right teams, and seeing customers in a true light. It happened by having the daring to step away from what everyone else was doing to create something unique, valuable, and commercially viable. It happened through courageous leadership and vision.

The Innovation Activation Plan

Nintendo's story and the stories of many of the companies and leaders we've talked about are filled with lessons and hope for a brighter future led by innovation. We hope that through their example and our guidance, this can be your story too. Rather than bring things to a close in this final chapter, we want to open the door to a new beginning; we want to activate *you* to write your own story.

Throughout the book, we've talked about what you need to know to integrate innovation with your strategy, leadership, and company. Now it's time to take those lessons and translate them into actionable thinking for your company. It begins with you and evolves into an ever-widening circle of inclusion from leader to company and from company to customer and back. Each successive step is meant to bring you closer to the ultimate prize: sustainable growth.

To help you do this, we've created what we call an "innovation activation plan." In it are five definitive steps that will serve as a road map to strengthen your innovation leadership and help you incorporate *Breaking Away*'s principles and frameworks into the DNA of your company.

For some of you, it may be a matter of making a few changes and adding some expanded thinking to your already-strong repertoire. For others, it will mean a major overhaul. Like Nintendo, you might even have to forge a path that no one else in your industry has been willing to take. Moving from today's company-centric focus to one that embraces innovation isn't easy. It means making a change in the core culture of the business, and it requires the participation of everyone, especially top leadership. It might not be painless, but it is possible. We've seen it, we've done it, and you can do it too.

Get Ready

In *The Art of War*, Sun Tzu taught, "The general who wins a battle makes many calculations in his temple ere the battle is fought. The general who loses a battle makes but few calculations beforehand." Preparation is the key to success in any contest, and in today's business world, winning the innovation war is the only way to break away and lead the pack. Whether you're a general or a CEO, you have to get ready.

Accept Accountability and Take Responsibility. "I am responsible." These are three of the most powerful words in the language of leadership. In fact, accepting the truth that you are ultimately accountable for who you are and what you do can be the single most defining moment of your career.

Leaders, more than anyone, need to accept responsibility for what they do, what they see, and how they influence those around them. When it comes to responsibility, it's our belief that leaders should actually be held to a *higher* standard. The reason for this is that given your position, influence, and authority, leaders like you affect so many lives that the consequences of your actions increase a hundredfold.

All leaders can be given accountability. They're certainly given authority. But no one can give another responsibility. That's something you have to take on and own. Leadership and the responsibility that comes with it is a choice; it's a mindset you accept. You don't *become* a leader because you have authority; you *are* a leader because of how you choose to use it.

Sometimes that means taking responsibility for events or out-comes you weren't involved in or that were outside your control. In fact, if you're involved in innovation, it's almost guaranteed that things will occur that are outside of your control. When they do, you don't wait for permission, worry about public opinion, or weigh your personal options. You act in the best interests of your company and your people. You support progress, and you act to make a difference.

When Isabel Noboa Ponton lost her father in 1994, it set in motion a series of events that would test even the most accomplished business magnate. Largely inexperienced in the corporate world, she was still her father's daughter and had learned much from him. When he died, Luis Noboa was a self-made billionaire who had turned banana exporting into an empire that included shipping, real estate, and banking. After exhausting negotiations with the family over the inheritance, Isabel eventually took $70 million and, with her husband, began building a 1-million-square-foot shopping center and business complex in her home in Guayaquil, Ecuador. Completed in 1997, the center was the largest on the South Pacific coast.

What should have been a cause for celebration soon turned sour. In 1998, struggling with a failing marriage, she took full control of the consortium. That same year, Ecuador's economy fell apart. The country's currency lost more than 88 percent of its value, ushering in the worst fiscal crisis in the nation's history. Facing a zero percent occupancy in her new project, Noboa took the bull by the horns. She rallied her employees and asked them to forgo pay raises until the crisis passed. In turn, she promised to be tireless in her efforts to turn things around. "We worked in teams," she says. "We assumed the responsibility and made a commitment not to fail the people depending on us. Everyone understood that these were not my companies, but ours." The hard work paid off. Since then, her real estate empire has expanded to include hotels and hospitals, and she's added a sugar mill and an interest in the Ecuador Coca-Cola Bottling Company to her portfolio of businesses, which are worth in excess of $500 million. Today, she is one of the most respected business figures in Ecuador.

Isabel could have blamed others for the troubles she experienced and given in to the pressures of what seemed to be an impossible situation, but she believes that accepting that kind of defeat is giving others the power to create (or destroy) your happiness and success. Accepting responsibility means that you refuse, even if it's from this moment on, to criticize or blame others for any reason. When you accept full responsibility for a situation, it means you have the power to create the solution. Most of the time, you do that anyway, don't you? Start taking credit for all your wonderful ideas by also taking responsibility when things go wrong. From now on, no matter what happens, say to yourself, "I am responsible."

If this isn't an area of strength for you, outline some initial steps for increasing accountability and a sense of responsibility in all areas, including innovation. Where can you make changes? Set priorities and timelines. Then make sure that others know the buck starts and ends with you. To ensure that you're on track, ask others to confirm that you've communicated your commitment clearly. People need to know intellectually, as well as feel, that you're leading them.

Identify Your Innovation Vision. Remember when you were a child and you'd make up stories of adventures or daydream about what you wanted to be when you grew up? That was your untethered right brain exploring possibilities. You need to tap into that same feeling again, because even though responsibility is the conscience of innovation leadership, vision is its soul. And what you need now is a vision.

In Chapter 1, we outlined the four levels of innovation: Transformational, Category, Marketplace, and Operational. We also said that to build sustainable growth, you need to be engaged in at least three of these levels at all times. Using this as a foundation, let's create a vision for your company that keeps innovation top of mind. To begin with, identify the overarching customer-driven focus that will guide innovation for your company. Nintendo wanted to bring simplicity and fun back to gaming; that was the vision that drove everything it did. Pacific Gas and Electric Company wanted to make power accessible and affordable. McCain Foods wanted to provide healthy, convenient products for professional and home-based chefs. When you have this kind of direction, it allows you to evaluate projects, operations, and channel performance to make sure all of them are focused on delivering the vision.

Once you've identified your vision, apply it to the four levels of innovation. Make a column for each level, then write down how you are—or how you should be—articulating your vision through innovation. If, for example, you're like Apple and your vision is simplicity, then making things simple as an innovation objective is something on which operations should be focused constantly. The same would be true of your Marketplace Innovations. What could you be doing in packaging, shopping, providing service, or solving problems to make things easy? If your primary function is to facilitate communications, do your innovations connect people or put layers of technology between you and your customers? From a customer perspective, there probably isn't anyone who doesn't rue the day automated answering systems were adopted. It might have been good for company operations, but the customer ended up losing. That's really the point of this exercise. To help you begin to see how customer, vision, and multilevel innovation work together. All three need to act in concert. Innovation driven by vision is innovation destined for greatness.

Connect Your Innovation Vision to Your Total Company Vision. Setting your vision based on the customer is critical, but if that vision doesn't also serve the company, it's not going to give you the alignment you need to drive growth. This is where the three Ws come into your activation plan. Not only can you work toward alignment for individual projects as we explained in Chapter 4, but you can do the same for the entire company and your innovation vision.

Building on the previous step, fill in your "who circle" with high-level insight about current and hoped-for customers. A new start-up called WePay is hoping to solve the problem of collecting money from groups such as class reunions, bachelor party attendees, or even roommates by allowing users to create group accounts. With this innovation that builds off the PayPal model, the group administrator can set the amount, due date, and other details and send out a bill or request for payment, then WePay collects the funds. Its potential audience is just about any group from a fantasy football league to a charity fundraiser or yoga studio.

Once you know the who, you need to state your business case in the "why circle." Why does this make business sense? What are the overarching needs of the company? WePay needs to increase its subscriber base and incremental revenue. McCain Foods needed to make a switch from supplying demand to creating it. What are your needs, and how can innovation provide the solution?

To answer that question, it helps to look at where you are in the business life cycle. Five phases can be applied to an offering, a division, a business, or a company as a whole. We've labeled these start-up, formative years, acceleration, maturity, and decline. Each phase has its own issues that innovation can address. In Table 10.1, we've listed some of the most pressing issues, along with the types of innovation (in order of importance) you should consider. Notice that Operational Innovation is listed in every phase of the cycle. That's because every company should be engaged continually in improving the running of the business. It's as simple as that.

After you identify where you are in the life cycle and who your customers are, you can address the "what circle." What problems are you trying to solve, or what advantages are you trying to provide through innovation? What technologies can you

TABLE 10.1 Business Life Cycle

PHASE	ISSUES	INNOVATION
Start-Up	Survival Getting customers Establishing a foothold	Transformational (this can be the impetus for a start-up) Category (new markets or applications are the basis for the business) Operational (setting up the most effective processes)
Formative Years	Accelerating growth Efficiency	Marketplace (new iterations can add revenue with little additional cost) Category (important for continued major growth and development) Operational (continually looking at how effective operational mechanisms are)
Acceleration	High revenue, low profit Low efficiency Little time to spare Overextended resources	Operational (important for increased profitability) Marketplace (important for quick new incremental growth) Category (important to keep things fresh and expanding) Transformational (critical to invest for the future now)

continued

PHASE	ISSUES	INNOVATION
Maturity	On a sales plateau Asleep in "comfort zone" Loss of passion Loss of older customers No new customers Fear of "rocking the boat"	Category (hopefully being developed on-going, establishes new customer bases) Marketplace (needed to keep things competitive and customer focused) Operational (continued focus for productivity) Transformational (*must* make investments to invent the future)
Decline	Loss of base Imminent layoffs Defeatist attitude	Marketplace (this may be a primary area to tide you over until larger-scale innovation takes hold) Category (needed to stop decline) Operational (can boost profits but not the sole solution) Transformational (if investments have been made here, they should start to take hold; if not, there is probably not time for them to stem the tide)

leverage? Look at the projects in your pipeline. Do they serve your vision and your customers? Do they align with your business life cycle phase and needs? What ideas come to mind that aren't in the pipeline but should be, based on customer insight? Maybe WePay could offer temporary Web pages for events as an added revenue stream. This would help the company survive and could also help grow its customer base. Jot down any ideas you have while you work through this step. Later, as you move further into your innovation activation plan, you can use this work to help you build your strategy and set your priorities.

Develop an Innovation Gap Analysis. Most people are familiar with the idea of a gap analysis. It's how you assess where you are against where you want to be. What's missing is the gap. With innovation, you need to focus on three areas to get a clear picture of your innovation readiness: leadership, environment, and pipeline.

Leadership. While the responsibility for innovation is ultimately yours, you still need leaders around you to help execute the vision, people with the right stuff. Throughout Part 2, we talked about the thinking style, characteristics, and capabilities of leadership, including specific profiles necessary for the different levels of innovation. Now that you've determined what your vision is and how that vision fits with your business strategy, you need to build your innovation team. Begin by creating a list of attributes from the profiles in Chapter 7 for each level of innovation you want to engage in. Also build a list of innovation-focused qualities you want everyone on your "leadership dream team" to have. Here are some examples:

- Is capable of whole-brain thinking
- Looks for a better way and challenges convention to generate ideas
- Connects the dots and recognizes adjacencies
- Can predict and moderate risk
- Motivates others
- Relates new ideas to existing business strategies
- Understands customer needs as they relate to a specific area
- Is committed to delivering exceptional customer experiences

Keep adding to this list until you have a good overview of what you're looking for. Then assess the people around you to see how close you are to the ideal. Do you have a good mix of big-picture category types, marketplace magicians, and nuts-and-bolts operational stewards? Do you need an internal transformational leader, or is that function best served from incubation or outside partnerships?

Earlier we talked about A. G. Lafley and how the Talent Portfolio he used tracked the top two hundred executives in his company. It was an exhaustive undertaking, but his commitment to developing the right kind of leaders to drive innovation was clear to everyone around him. Great leaders demand great leadership. That's why many of the people we've talked about did some serious housecleaning when they took over. In several cases, more than a third of the executive staff turned over in the first year or two. When the dust settled, what emerged was a cohesive team focused on one vision and one goal: sustainable growth through innovation.

Environment. Environment, or the culture of your business, is next on the list. We've talked about the importance of culture in innovation throughout the leadership section and in depth in Chapter 8. Innovation can thrive only if it's nurtured, and it can be nurtured only by caring enough about the people you lead to see them as people of worth. They are your responsibility, so caring enough about them to offer the best environment in which to work is part of that responsibility.

Your task here is to envision what you see as the ideal culture for innovation. If we were doing so, some of the things we'd include would be providing an inspiring physical space, intellectual stimulation, personal and professional enrichment, freedom to create, accountability, and personal responsibility. The list can be as long as you like, and the picture as detailed as necessary. Let your right brain take over. When you're done, compare your ideal to your reality. How different are they? What's standing in the way of turning what you wish into what you live?

Make a list and rank the entries from simple to difficult to fix, then pledge to set a timeline for change and share it with your people. If you need some inspiration, go back and read about Peter Darbee at PG&E in Chapter 2. He did what we're asking you to do, as did Burberry's Ahrendts, Nintendo's Iwata, and Bill Ford. We know it can be done with astonishing success. People are the heartbeat of innovation. Creating a culture that supports it may be the single most important legacy you can leave your company.

Pipeline. With your ideal leadership team and innovation culture identified, the final step is evaluating your pipeline. To do this, you'll need to see how well your innovation ideas or projects align with the who, what, and why you've identified and whether or not they support your overall vision and innovation strategy. This can be a real eye-opener. Sometimes you find that a favorite project is completely wrong for the company or an idea that seemed to be "no big deal" ends up being a major game changer.

With the economy recently putting a damper on spending, retailers have been flailing around, trying to get people shopping again. Stores have tried everything from deep price cuts to megastar designer lines, mostly to no avail. Nordstrom's, which is world renowned for customer service, has beaten the odds by changing, of all things, how it handles inventory. It melded website and store inventory into one giant, transparent shopping experience, and people love it. This might not seem revolutionary, but it's a rarity in the retailing world.

With this new system, Nordstrom's shoppers can see an item online, determine whether it's available at a nearby store, reserve it, and pick it up the same day. If you see something online and the only one available is sitting on a Nordstrom's shelf three hundred miles away, an associate can ship it to you. If the company hadn't linked and displayed all its inventory online at once, sales like that could never happen. "This change drove some pretty meaningful results," says Jamie Nordstrom, president of Nordstrom Direct. In fact, an August 23, 2010, *New York Times* article reported that Nordstrom's was the department store with one of the most improved same-store sales over the last year. In just eleven months, its same-store sales increased an average of 8 percent versus an 11.9 percent decrease the previous year.

Of note is the fact that this innovation is perfectly aligned with the company's vision of delivering the best customer service in the business, while at the same time it increases revenues. Price cuts wouldn't have done it, and neither would more designer labels. When looking at your pipeline, ask yourself how well your projects fit your innovation strategy, then weed out anything that doesn't belong and fast-track those that have the greatest potential based on risk analysis.

Once you've completed your evaluation, assign projects to the appropriate innovation level to make sure you have a good mix. Are you loaded down with Operational Innovations but light on the marketplace front? Do you need to jump into Category Innovation, either on your own or in collaboration with another company or group? As we've said often, Transformational Innovation isn't for everyone, but you should still keep an eye on what's out there to see where follow-on opportunities might be. Make sure your team includes transformational exploration in its long-term strategy. Speaking of strategy, with this final piece of your gap analysis in place, you should have a good sense of your innovation readiness. So now it's time to go from what you *might* do to what you *will* do.

Get Set

If Sun Tzu were continuing to coach us, he might say, "Now that you've asked the questions, reflected on the answers, and assessed your strengths and weaknesses, it's time to make a plan." He would be right. Creating an innovation strategy is something every company, regardless of size, industry, or business cycle, should put on the top of its priority list. Without an innovation strategy, even your best plans nearly always end up being nothing more than a conversation that never moves forward. You can't be serious about innovation, or expect others to be serious about it, if you don't commit to it in writing. You've seen the vision; now it's time to take it to the drawing board.

Creating an Innovation Strategy. One of the issues we have with current business thinking is the practice of using one-size-fits-all processes, especially when it comes to innovation. Every business has its own personality and way of doing things, and every CEO needs to put his or her personal stamp on the vision being nurtured. That's why *Breaking Away* was presented as a framework from which to create your own unique spin on innovation. While having an innovation strategy is critical, how you create it is up to you. Use a process that's familiar and comfortable for you and your people. Have a good balance of blue sky and real-world orientation, and above all, use your whole brain! We'd also like to suggest that you include the following steps to make sure your plan propels, rather than sinks, your innovation mission.

1. Set Innovation Priorities. There isn't a company in existence whose resources aren't finite. That means you have to make the most of yours by focusing on problems you're uniquely equipped to solve and opportunities you're uniquely placed to exploit. This means setting priorities. As you build your plan, make sure to set and prioritize goals in these critical areas: (1) innovation brainstorming, risk management, funding, and alignment; (2) leadership synergy, development, collaboration, and accountability; and (3) activation of the company and customer through culture and communication.

Consider what will serve the company in the short term, while keeping a focused eye on long-term innovation. Both are necessary for success. Perhaps an innovation priority might be more effective dissemination of new technologies, processes, and ideas to increase innovation across the company, or maybe it's a commitment to foster industries of the future. A leadership goal might be a commitment that asks each associate to be accountable for driving at least one innovation change per year. In the activation area, you might develop a culture of collaboration, not only internally, but also between research, industry, and academia. If you set priorities based on the three pillars of innovation, leadership, and activation, you'll be assured that no one area is ignored to the detriment of your overall growth.

2. Establish Success Metrics. As important as innovation is to success, surprisingly only about a third of Fortune 1000 companies have formal innovation metrics. Of those that do, there's really no consensus about best practices. The reason for this isn't lack of trying. Entire consultancies are built around the issue. The more likely culprit is innovation itself. It's just not that easy to pin down.

Metrics, by their very nature, are defined by numbers. As hard as we sometimes try, however, innovation can't—or more accurately *shouldn't be*—reduced to digits, at least not entirely. When numbers are driving innovation, then numbers and a large dose of caution, not inspired ideas, are what you get back. On the other hand, using only soft measures like success stories, leadership engagement, or improvement in workplace attitudes isn't enough either. Just like innovation itself, metrics are best achieved through a whole-brain approach. That means using qualitative (right-brain) and quantitative (left-brain) measures applied to innovation, leadership, and culture.

Look at what factors drive return on investment (ROI). Specifically, identify what increases positive business returns and what reduces necessary investment. Also consider how much capital is being invested in innovation-focused actions like presenting and developing ideas for the pipeline. Then determine the actual result of these efforts. Since sourcing ideas and technology from the outside is becoming increasingly important to maintain a healthy innovation flow, there could be a significant financial impact from royalties, intellectual property, and licensing. Remember JVC, which licensed its technology early on, bringing in billions in royalties.

When developing your own financial metrics, keep in mind that dollars are only one part of innovation. Don't forget that Transformational and, in many cases, Category Innovations should be subject to different measures. It could be years before an ROI can even be determined. On these long-term projects, think more in terms of milestones reached and lessons learned. ROI measures are important; they give innovation management fiscal discipline and help justify the value of strategic initiatives. But they can't be the sole basis for determining the success of your innovation strategy.

In addition to financial metrics, look at cultural metrics. Figure out how well cultural change initiatives have worked by seeing if there is increased workforce participation in innovation and evaluating what barriers still exist. For example, 3M allows employees to spend up to 15 percent of their time exploring new opportunities. In return, it expects 35 percent of its revenue to come from new products introduced within the past four years.[5] Quantitative measures in this area can be activity oriented, such as how many people are participating in innovation efforts and what percentage of people have had training specifically related to innovation readiness and activation. Tie qualitative metrics to success stories on workplace-based changes or employee/

customer interaction or activation. Innovation is about inspiration, so it's important to share inspiring stories that help to generate it.

The final measure we'd like you to consider is in the leadership area. These metrics should address the behaviors that senior management and leaders must demonstrate in order to support a culture of innovation. Include accountability for specific growth initiatives. How much time do executives spend on strategic innovation versus day-to-day operations? How much training have they received specific to innovation, including risk assessment, innovation alignment, and pipeline development? If the company is doing its job in developing innovation leaders, a good percentage of them should become leaders of new-category businesses. When those you've mentored move up, this also becomes a measure of your overall success.

Whatever process you develop, make sure it's done with the involvement and buy-in of your key stakeholders. The people who have to live by the metrics should be a part of setting and evolving them. Make metric reviews an ongoing process that captures insights from your organization's successes and failures. As an integrated part of your innovation strategy, metrics can be a valuable indicator of how innovation-centric you really are. If used properly, they can also be just the incentive you need to turn an ego-centric culture into a one-for-all-and-all-for-one powerhouse.

3. Develop Clear Communications. When London was literally flattened by fire in 1666, Christopher Wren, one of the country's greatest architects, was commissioned to rebuild St. Paul's Cathedral. A massive undertaking, it required inspired vision, tons of stone, and hundreds of men to bring it to life. The story goes that one day in 1671, Wren was surveying the project when he came across three masons working on scaffolding. One was crouched down working on a stone block. Wren asked him what he was doing.

The man replied, "Making a living."

The next man was putting a stone in place, and Wren asked him the same question, "What, sir, are you doing?"

"Building a wall," the man replied.

Finally, Wren turned to the third man, who was standing and shouldering a massive stone brick. When the architect asked him the same question, the man stood a little taller and replied, "I'm working with the Master Wren, sir, and we're building a great cathedral for the glory of the Almighty."

There's a great lesson for all of us in this story. If you want to know just how effective your communications are, ask your people what they're doing. If they don't know they're helping to build a cathedral, then you, like most of your peers, need to make innovation communications a more integral part of your strategic plan. Despite the current explosion of communication tools, innovation strategy—with its goals, commitment, and holistic involvement—is one of the most poorly communicated initiatives in most companies.

This is due, in part, to the overload of messages people receive every day. With so much to filter through, how is anyone supposed to know what's important? Innovation communication also suffers from what Bilal calls "flavor of the month syndrome," where management announces a new program or initiative and either never follows up on it or doesn't provide the necessary funding to see it through. To make sure people know what's going on, what's expected of them, and what their part in the overall vision is, you need to keep them consistently informed in a meaningful and useful way.

Market research shows that a message needs to be repeated at least seven times before someone really understands it and puts it into practice. When you communicate with a consistent, transparent message, you'll begin to see changes in employee behavior that reflect your management commitment to deliver on the innovation vision. In fact, for Joseph Tucci, chief executive officer of EMC Corp., the number-one data storage solution company in the world, there's nothing more important than communication.

In a *Business Management* interview, he talked about the success his company has enjoyed even through the recession. He attributes a great deal of that success to keeping everyone a part of the process openly and honestly. "You have to communicate a balance of reality and honesty, with vision, strategy, and proof points built in," he says. "'If we do X, this is what's going to happen. If we do Y, this will happen.' You honestly address the reality of the situation. 'I thought this would happen, but we fared even better that that.' Or 'I thought this would happen, but we fell a little short for these reasons; here's what we're going to do about it.' You have to be very open, and I don't care where you're from in the world, people react to that. If they think for a second that you're giving them spin, you've lost them."[6]

This kind of transparency is critical to innovation engagement. As part of your strategy, develop a planned corporate communications program that reaches all levels. Stress the importance of innovation and each individual's place in the strategic framework of the company. Be consistent and constant over a long period of time, and use a variety of communication channels, including e-mails, meetings, corporate magazines and newsletters, video clips, and even the company's social networking sites like Facebook. In addition to keeping everyone informed, involved, and engaged, constant communication sets the stage for reviewing strategic plans, evaluating projects, and setting expectations about the importance of innovation throughout the organization. In other words, you won't just have a company of bricklayers. You'll have a unified community of artisans.

Go

From the first page of *Breaking Away*, our goal has been to bring you to the point where you can make innovation come to life with a language and framework that informs your thinking and inspires your entire organization. Our job has been to point the way and outline the steps to get you started on the right path. Even with a well-crafted plan, we don't pretend it will be easy. For many companies, focusing on innovation will require enormous change. But even if you start small, one positive step forward will lead to another. From there, you can activate buy-in from your stakeholders. Ask everyone to embrace innovation, to change for the better. As you communicate your strategy, listen and learn from reactions. Where is the enthusiasm, and where is the confusion? Let people, not just numbers, guide you and adjust as needed.

Be sure to establish a way to incorporate both internal and external feedback loops. Innovation is a never-ending process of discovery and evolution that, at its best, creates products, services, and companies that are unique, valuable, and worthy of exchange. This is the true test of innovation. Everything you do should be judged against it. It's crucial to constantly ask whether any given strategy is unique, valuable, and worthy of exchange. If it's not, it's not innovation; and if it's not innovation, it's not serving your long-term sustainable growth.

Finally, as you plan to implement your innovation strategy, remember that victories inspire and build buy-in, so identify steps you can take that show the merit of an innovation focus. Weigh the rewards and sacrifices of your early efforts and make sure they're balanced. Experiencing success will make it easier to continue the process until you reach your goal of being a true innovation company. It won't happen overnight. But it is possible, as countless companies have already proven.

Those whose stories we've told in these pages have, knowingly or not, begun making innovation in who and what they're about. They started by keeping the customer first and foremost on everyone's mind and looking for ways to make life better. We know it's uncomfortable giving up old dictates that tell us business is about profits above all else or standing up to pressure for short-term gains in order to ensure long-term prosperity. In fact, there is very little about innovation that is comfortable. But as companies like Nintendo, General Electric, Ford, McCain Food, Teva, Hasbro, Burberry, Emirates Airlines, and so many others that have embraced innovation have shown, the rewards far outweigh the pain. Debate about innovation has been around for decades, but it's still the path less traveled. It's our hope this won't be the case for long.

Notes

Chapter 1

1. E. Phillip Krider, "Benjamin Franklin and Lightning Rods," *Physics Today*, January 2006, 45.
2. Interviews with Bruno Jactel, August 2010.
3. Interview Notes from Bill Ford, September 1, 2010.
4. "Steve Jobs's Commencement Speech at Stanford," Scribd, June 12, 2005, http://www.scribd.com/doc/1313/Steve-Jobss-Commencement-Speech-at-Stanford (accessed October 20, 2010).
5. Keith Barry, "Ford Bets the Fiesta on Social Networking," *Wired*, April 17, 2009, http://www.wired.com/autopia/2009/04/how-the-fiesta (accessed October 20, 2010).
6. "Michael Dell: Thinking Outside the Box," *Bloomberg BusinessWeek*, November 22, 2004, http://www.businessweek.com/magazine/content/04_47/b3909024_mz072.htm (accessed March 3, 2010).
7. Ibid.
8. "Why Circuit City Failed, and Why B & H Thrives," *Inc.*, http://www.inc.com/magazine/20090501/why_circuit_city_failed_and_why_bh_thrives_Printer_Friendly.html _ (accessed February 12, 2010).

Chapter 2

1. Anthony Hallett and Diane Hallett, *Entrepreneur Magazine Encyclopedia of Entrepreneurs* (New York: John Wiley & Sons, 1997), 170–72.
2. Ibid.
3. "Adam Grosser and His Sustainable Fridge," TED interview, February 2007, http://www.ted.com/talks/adam_grosser_and_his_sustainable_fridge.html (accessed March 22, 2010).
4. "About Sara," Spanx, 2010, http://www.spanx.com/corp/index.jsp?page=sarasStory&clickId=sarasstory_aboutsara_text (accessed November 29, 2010).
5. "P&G's AG Lafley on Innovation," video interview, *Bloomberg Business-Week* [no date given], http://feedroom.businessweek.com/?fr_story=907b67debd8cfaa2bcb64ba97265d4e7a08bcfeb (accessed March 12, 2010).
6. Interview with Brian Goldner, 2010.
7. Andy Reinhardt, "Skype's 'Aha!' Experience," *BusinessWeek*, September 19, 2005, http://www.businessweek.com/print/technogloy/content/sept2005/tc20050919_2468.htm (accessed May 11, 2010).
8. James Gosling, "The Skype Guys," *Time*, April 30, 2006, http://www.time.com/time/printout/0,8816,1187489,00.html (accessed May 11, 2010).

9. Mike Harvey, "Skype Could Be Cut Off for Good over Dispute," Times-Online, July 31, 2009, http://business.timesonline.co.uk/tol/business/indus try_sectors/technology/article6735381.ece (accessed May 12, 2010).

10. Geoffrey A. Fowler and Cassell Bryan-Low, "eBay Sells Skype to Investor Group," *The Wall Street Journal*, September 2, 2009, http://online.wsj.com/article/SB12517967665375495.hml (accessed May 11, 2010).

Chapter 3

1. Steve Rothwell and Andrea Rothman, with Cornelius Rahn, "Emirates Wins with Big Planes and Low Costs," *Bloomberg BusinessWeek*, July 5–July 11, 2010, 18–19.

2. Ibid.

Chapter 4

1. Interview with Martin Glenn, 2009.

2. "A History of the Potato Chip," The Nibble, http://www.thenibble.com/reviews/main/snacks/chip-history.asp (accessed April 20, 2010).

3. "Laura Scudder," Wikipedia, July 25, 2010, http://en.wikipedia.org/wiki/Laura_Scudder (accessed November 14, 2010).

4. "Legacy of Leadership: Herman Warden Lay," South Carolina Business Hall of Fame, 2002, http://www.knowitall.org/legacy/laureates/Herman%20 Warden%20Lay.html (accessed April 25, 2010).

5. "Potato Chip," Wikipedia, November 13, 2010, http://en.wikipedia.org/wiki/Potato_chip (accessed November 14, 2010).

Part 2

1. Paul Sloane," Idea Receptiveness Survey" [no date provided], http://www.leader-values.com/Content/detail.asp?ContentDetailID=1244 (accessed November 29, 2010).

2. David Brooks, "In Praise of Dullness," *The New York Times*, May 18, 2009, http://www.nytimes.com/2009/05/19/opinion/19brooks.html (accessed November 27, 2010).

3. Ibid.

Chapter 5

1. Elana Holzman and Kevin Mannix, "Teva Reports Record Full Year 2009 and Fourth Quarter Results," Teva, February 16, 2010, http://www.teva pharm.com/pr/2010/pr_905.asp (accessed October 21, 2010).

2. Thomas Wren, *The Leader's Companion: Insights on Leadership Through the Ages* (New York, The Free Press, 1995).

3. "Biography of Jacques Nasser," Business.com [no date given], http://www.ref erenceforbusiness.com/biography/M-R/Nasser-Jacques-1947.html (accessed July 8, 2010).

4. Andrew English, "Volvo Sale: The End of Ford's Dream Showroom," *The Telegraph*, December 2, 2008, http://www.telegraph.co.uk/motoring/news/3541886/Volvo-sale-the-end-of-Fords-dream-showroom.html (accessed July 8, 2010).
5. "Biography of Jacques Nasser."
6. Ibid.
7. Joe DeMatio, "2010 Man of the Year: Alan Mulally, CEO, Ford Motor Company," *Automobile Magazine*, November 2009, http://www.automobilemag.com/features/awards/1001_2010_man_of_the_year_alan_mulally_ceo_ford_motor_company/index.html (accessed July 8, 2010).
8. Interview with Bill Ford, January 25, 2010.
9. Alex Taylor III, "How Toyota Lost Its Way," *Fortune*, July 12, 2010, http://money.cnn.com/2010/07/12/news/international/toyota_recall_crisis_full_version.fortune/index.htm (accessed July 15, 2010).
10. "The Toyota Way," Wikipedia, August 19, 2010, http://en.wikipedia.org/wiki/The_Toyota_Way (accessed November 14, 2010).
11. Taylor, "How Toyota Lost Its Way."
12. "John Sculley," Wikipedia, November 1, 2010, http://en.wikipedia.org/wiki/John_Sculley (accessed November 14, 2010).
13. "Apple's iMac a Sales Hit: Firm's Market Share Doubles Thanks to It," *Cincinnati Enquirer*, December 22, 1998.
14. Faith Arner, "Pass Go and Collect the Job of CEO," *BusinessWeek*, August 4, 2003, http://www.businessweek.com/print/magazine/contet/03_31/b3844091.htm (accessed July 8, 2010).

Chapter 6

1. Patricia Zacharias, "Henry Ford and Thomas Edison — A Friendship of Giants," *The Detroit News,* August 7, 1996 (accessed November 27, 2010).
2. Ibid.
3. Dan Eden, "Left Brain/Right Brain," ViewZone, 2006, http://viewzone2.com/bicamx.html (accessed October 21, 2010).
4. Diana LaSalle and Terry Brittain, *Priceless: Turning Ordinary Products into Extraordinary Experiencs* (Boston: Harvard Business School Press, 2002), 9–10.

Chapter 7

1. Interview with Dean Kamen, June 29, 2010.
2. Business Wire, "Bandai America Appoints Brian Goldner to Chief Operating Officer; Marketing Leadership and Vision Help Company Reach Highest Revenues in Four Years," The Free Library, August 19, 1999, http://www.thefreelibrary.com/Bandai+America+Appoints+Brian+Goldner+to+Chief+Operating+Officer%3B...-a055498034 (accessed July 8, 2010).
3. Maysa Rawi, "London Fashion Week: Burberry Makes History with World's First Star-Studded Catwalk Streamed Live in 3D," *Daily Mail*, February 24, 2010, http://www.dailymail.co.uk/femail/article-1253171/London-Fashion-Week-Burberry-set-stream-worlds-catwalk-live-3D.html (accessed July 10, 2010).

4. Robert Berner, "P&G: New and Improved," *BusinessWeek*, July 7, 2003, http://www.businessweek.com/print/magazine/content/03_27/b3840001 _mz001.htm?chan+gl (accessed July 8, 2010).
5. Noel Tichy, "AG Lafley, Judgement, and the Re-do Loop," *Harvard Business Review* blogs, June 12, 2009, http://blogs.hbr.org/now-new-next/2009/06/ag -lafley-judgment-and-the-red.html (accessed November 14, 2010).
6. "Mr. Clean Car Wash Eyes Expansion," Happi (Household and Personal Products Industry), February 2, 2010, http://www.happi.com/news/ 2010/02/10/mr._clean_car_wash_eyes_expansion (accessed July 8, 2010).
7. Jennifer Reingold, "CEO Swap: The $79 Billion Plan," *Fortune*, November 19, 2009, http://money.cnn.com/2009/11/19/news/companies/procter_gamble _lafley.fortune (accessed July 8, 2010).
8. Ibid.
9. Ibid.

Chapter 8

1. Jennifer Reingold, "CEO Swap: The $79 Billion Plan," *Fortune*, November 19, 2009, http://money.cnn.com/2009/11/19/news/companies/procter_gamble _lafley.fortune (accessed July 8, 2010).
2. "Jobs and Careers: Working at Ferrari," Ferrari, 2010, http://www.ferrari .com/English/about_ferrari/Jobs_Careers/Pages/Jobs_Careers.aspx (accessed November 14, 2010).
3. Stanford Graduate School of Business, "Customer Focus Keeps Amazon Experimenting, Bezos Says," *Stanford GSB News*, October 2003, http:// www.gsb.stanford.edu/mews/headlines/vftt_bezos.shtml (accessed October 21, 2010).
4. "Jobs and Careers: Working at Ferrari."
5. Robert Berner, "P&G: New and Improved," *BusinessWeek*, July 7, 2003, http://www.businessweek.com/print/magazine/content/03_27/b3840001 _mz001.htm?chan+gl (accessed July 8, 2010).
6. Ibid.

Chapter 9

1. Amy Gunderson, "The Great Leaders Series: Ruth Handler, Co-Founder of Mattel," *Inc.*, May 1, 2009, http://www.inc.com/30years/articles/ruth-handler .html (accessed November 14, 2010).
2. "Ruth & Elliot Handler Interview," YouTube [no date given], http://www.you tube.com/watch?v=X74R36qMJUM&feature=related (accessed November 14, 2010).
3. "Corporations: All's Swell at Mattel," *Time*, November 26, 1962, http://www .time.com/time/printout/0,8816,874558,00.html (accessed August 25, 2010).
4. "Brand Idea Failures: RJ Reynolds' Smokeless Cigarettes," Brand Idea Failures and Lessons Learned blog, November 25, 2006, http://brandfailures .blogspot.com/2006/11/brand-idea-failures-rj-reynolds.html (accessed August 25, 2010).

5. "Brand Extension Failures: Gerber Singles," Brand Extensions and Lessons Learned blog, December 1, 2006, http://brandfailures.blogspot.com/2006/12/brand-extension-failure-gerber-singles.html (accessed August 25, 2010).

6. Vanessa L. Facenda, "Mass Merchants Face Up to Higher End Skincare," *All Business*, January 1, 2004, http://www.allbusiness.com/retail-trade/4301607-1.html (accessed August 27, 2010).

7. "Olay," Wikipedia, November 11, 2010, http://en.wikipedia.org/wiki/Olay (accessed November 14, 2010).

8. Dave Owen, "The Betamax vs VHS Format War," MediaCollege.com, May 1, 2005, http://www.mediacollege.com/video/format/compare/betamax-vhs.html (accessed November 14, 2010).

9. "The Videotape Format Wars," Wikipedia, October 16, 2010, http://en.wikipedia.org/wiki/Videotape_format_war (accessed November 14, 2010).

10. Charlie Sorrel, "Apple's iPad Sales Accelerate: Three Million Sold in 80 Days," *Wired*, June 23, 2010, http://www.wired.com/gadgetlab/2010/06/apples-ipad-sales-accelerate-three-million-sold-in-80-days (accessed August 27, 2010).

11. "SAS® Analytics Test Effectiveness of Variety of Amazon.com Features" [no date given], http://www.crm2day.com/content/t6_librarynews_1.php?id=EEppElEkVuBHCMBqjb (accessed November 14, 2010).

12. Courtland Jenkins and Geoff Tuff, "Excellence in Market Activation," Monitor, January 28, 2009, http://www.monitor.com/Expertise/BusinessIssues/MarketingandPricing/tabid/66/ctl/ArticleDetail/mid/685/CID/20092701142028527/CTID/1/L/en-US/Default.aspx (accessed August 8, 2010).

Chapter 10

1. IGN Staff, "Profile: Satoru Iwata," IGN GameCube, July 16, 2002, http://cube.ign.com/articles/530/530986p1.html (accessed August 23, 2010).

2. Ibid.

3. James Rivington, "Wii Sends Nintendo Profits into Orbit," TechRadar UK, July 25, 2007, http://www.techradar.com/news/gaming/consoles/wii-sends-nintendo-profits-into-orbit-161327 (accessed August 23, 2010).

4. Daisuke Wakabayashi, "Nintendo Posts Full-Year Profit Drop," *The Wall Street Journal*, May 6, 2010, http://online.wsj.com/article/SB10001424052748704370704575227531691106498.html?mod=WSJ_Tech_LEFTTopNews (accessed November 14, 2010).

5. "Employee Engagement," 3M, 2010, http://solutions.3m.com/wps/portal/3M/zh_CN/global/sustainability/our-people/employee-engagement (accessed October 21, 2010).

6. "Joseph Tucci of EMC," *Business Management*, issue 19 [no date given], http://www.busmanagement.com/article/Joseph-Tucci-of-EMC (accessed August 23, 2010).

Index